THE QUIRKY LANDLORD

All I want is a room somewhere....away

from the cold night air, Eliza Doolittle,

My Fair Lady

Clancy Rohring

ISBN: 1492980242
ISBN 13: 9781492980247
Library of Congress Control Number: 2013920062
CreateSpace Independent Publishing Platform
North Charleston, South Carolina

I. The Road to Landlordism

CHAPTER ONE

The Past

1955

In my senior year in high school, I, Clancy Rohring, danced two dances at lunch hour with Jordan Charles, my rally partner. Swing style, not close. Photos of it were taken for the yearbook. A wonderful dancer, Jordan was the only African American in the junior class. A teacher, in charge of student activities, Al Fedje, closed down the extra large room the next day "for storage."

In 1968 the Speech teacher told me I got the most votes for the historic Portland Rose Festival. "The Mormon students, a teacher in real estate, and Mr. Fedje were so rabid about the dance in 1955, a teachers committee chose Nancy Craft. She was introduced as the students' choice. The next year Mr. Fedje left education to fundraise for the conservative American Heritage Foundation," he concluded.

1957

I sponsored the first minority member of my sorority at the University of Oregon. Judging by the flak I attracted for doing so, Janice Nakata, second-generation Japanese, was probably the first female minority member of any Greek organization nationwide.

1960

Overnight on Wake Island, as a Pan Am stew on the Boeing Stratocruiser, I scoured the atoll for bazookas, disturbed earth, and signs of other life as part of a special team. At Guam the piston aircraft picked up more military personnel. In Manila, with the Pan Am employees showing only our crew cards, security let us in the back door to the hall that led to the banquet room of the Manila Hotel. We watched President Eisenhower transit the hallway only ten feet away. It was May, and he was headed to the first free nations economic conference in Tokyo.

In a Boeing 707, in force since January, crossing Fiji on the way to Sydney, billows of smoke reached the flight, thirty thousand feet up. The captain took the plane down to investigate. When the door opened, the stench was god-awful, inhumane, not merely from scorched indigo fields. The cockpit crew, armed to the hilt, exited and shut the door after them. The cabin crew did not look out the windows because the shades were pulled. The crew never uttered a sound when they returned. I asked no questions. **An explanation was never provided.**

1965

I, Clancy Bloch, taught world history at a NASA junior high, Clear Creek, thirty miles south of Houston. Gus Grissom's son was in my ninth grade class. In December 1964 I had taught all black juniors (the class was not integrated) in the Houston Public Schools as a substitute teacher. Unseen persons in the hallway would snicker and utter the word "Pinky," a derogatory term for the racially mixed. At that time in the South, white teachers did not teach black classes.

In late spring the University of Texas alums of my sorority invited me to a gathering in a Houston hotel suite. Barbara and George H. W. Bush were there. He had just lost the Harris County election to Yarborough. The guests seemed to know a lot about me.. The sorority sisters admonished me for working while pregnant.

Brad Bloch, my spouse, a devout Republican, would later often brag, "The president mixed me a drink in Houston." Immediately following that "historic" event, Brad cajoled with serious intent, "If you're so open-minded, Clancy, join the Republican Party and see how the other half lives." I had failed to vote for Goldwater.

In December God gave me a beautiful, healthy son who could see and talk to me, when I first held him. I named him Herbert, after my beloved grandfather, who was my confidant and mentor from age seven, when my father died.

1966

As a graduate assistant at Portland State's History Department, my thesis was "The Soviet Role in the Korean Conflict: The Sino-Soviet Treaty of 1950," and Soviet influence on the Chinese particularly bothered me.

In March the Dorcester Conference, organized by Bob Packwood, attracted liberal Republicans. I gave the Foreign Relations Committee's report to the convention floor. My theme: "Let us give Chinese students an alternative to Moscow University." I proposed *U.S. Recognition of the Chinese People's Republic,"* to counteract the singular Soviet dominance in that country. It was put to a vote and carried the floor with only two nays. Tall Governor Tom McCall stood above the crowd. His vote was not one of the two nays.

While working on Packwood's US Senate campaign, a bigwig from Cheney's state of Wyoming who'd graduated from Willamette University kicked me out of the party. As a volunteer when I telephoned headquarters for another assignment for mostly clerical work, Jo Simpson asked, me, "Are you trying to destroy the party?"Mrs. Simpson, wife of Packwood's campaign manager, didn't give me a chance to answer. My name was removed from all lists. I became a nonperson as far as the Republican Party was concerned.

I can only suspect that my proposal for recognition of China was objected to by some power people in the party. Even Bob Packwood, later quoted, was not hot at the time on recognition of communist China. Nevertheless, he did abide by Roberts Rules of Order to bring my proposal to a vote.

The Republican president, Richard Nixon, did go to China in 1972. It was heralded as his one brilliant political move.

CHAPTER TWO

The Future

1996

I telephoned Lacey Latrop because she sent me a get-well card for no reason. "I'm not sick, Lacey," I told her.

"Oh my gosh, Clancy," she gushed. "Brad said you weren't at the Raffetys' wedding because you were not feeling well. He said, 'She's that way' and pointed to his head."

That suggests I'm looney, I thought. "I didn't know about the Raffety wedding," I blurted. Guarded, I continued, "Since 1989 I've been working sixty-plus hours, one and a half jobs per week, to keep things going, keep in touch with our son, Herb and his wife, build retirement. Do you know I even quit smoking? It saves a lot, and I feel great!"

"We've missed you," Lacey said softly but cautiously.

What the hell? I thought. Brad's favorite saying: *"What appears to be is more important than what is."* There's no more quandary. I don't feel anything anymore except fear—of him.

In 1968 I'd seen a divorce attorney. The jerk sent the bill to our house. My husband intercepted it. Brad had shoved me around and threatened, "You divorce me and you'll never see your son again."

I'd believed him.

CHAPTER THREE
Professional!

In reality, the loss of my dream job had less to do with that new female CEO coming in, although femaleness is totally to blame for it. I say female because it has been my experience that females, on the whole, are more authoritarian than men. They're accustomed to bossing little kids around and insist on "no sass back." Moreover, they're inclined (most of them) to kick out of the nest any arbitrators or nonconformists. Or is it mostly just authority, male or female, making vile decisions for the rest of us?

Karlene, a friend of mine, a man who'd become a woman, left a very wealthy home at sixteen, worked his/her way through college, and never returned. The stepmother who was the total control freak wrote him/her off. How many young people struggling with their "gayness" or sexuality get bad advice or utter rejection from mama? The female has the last say-so. Anything short of that is rape. Even after her consent, it can still be construed as rape. The female has long claimed a right to change her mind.

In short, I failed the office politics test dominated by three accounting clerks, one payroll clerk, one assistant to the plant/operations manager, and one administrative assistant, all female. The administrative assistant was hired by corporate in 1996 to handle group manager Frank Clausen's correspondence and phone calls.

Corporate acquisitions in Denver shortly took my beloved manager out of town extensively and put Jeannette Stork, the administrative assistant—who was shortly given the additional title of human resources manager—in charge, mostly because the comptroller and the sales manager were now both on the road. The plant manager as well as the assistant manager had other duties.

The only independent female voice in the office was the oversize (four pancakes with strawberry compote and whipped cream, sausage, bacon, and ham; three eggs sunny-side up, hash browns, and toast; oatmeal with brown sugar, raisins, and half and half; orange juice; banana fritters; a chocolate chip muffin; and a side order of french fries for breakfast out with the office staff) Bess Browley. She didn't know she was pregnant until it was time to deliver since she had never had intercourse, verbal or sexual, with the opposite sex in her entire life. She was a two-ton Tessie and struggled mostly with how to acquire vittles and consume them.

Nevertheless, she was a very valuable employee and did the very accurate job of three persons for a starting minimum wage. Her high school records revealed a 160 IQ. She supported her unemployed parents and, with the son she brought forth, qualified for a house by Habitat for Humanity. Even though the state authorities badgered her for a name of the sperm-carrier, she never gave vent to the temptation to just grab up on some poor fellow she disliked. Rather she insisted on her "nobody."

That set Bess further apart from the norm than ever before, into the category of "mentally unstable" at the least. When she was on her computer, as I passed by her cubicle I would hear her sing, "Jesus loves me, yes I know, the Bible tells me so" again and again.

When the comptroller, Rick Bondsted, saw me in that vicinity, he told me to stay away from her. "Don't talk to her," he said.

I asked, "Why?"

He insisted, "She has very important work to do. Not to be interrupted."

After the comptroller's indifference, I remained curious. I got the explanation of what had happened to her and Bess's background which I have just explained from Kit, my friend in Inventory (now located in the plant), who regularly had breakfast with the accounting and billing crew every Monday. Kit used to be manager of customer service but was sent to Inventory to make room for a customer service manager from the Australia plant who was married to the new service manager coming in. It was a time when old faces I could count on—my so-called support system—were disappearing.

8

My office was as small as a clothes closet, but I took great pride in it. It set me apart from the large room where the other females gathered. The sales staff had moved to a new facility near the airport, but the design did not include an office for Marketing because Marketing was "officially" only at the corporate office in Burbank. That physical arrangement led to a further distrust of my value, conjured up by the clerks in Accounting.

My mother had passed away in 1995 and left us—my brother, sister, and myself, plus the Sisters of Providence—$17,000 each. For $12,000 cash I purchased a 1997 Honda Civic from the fleet manager at Beaverton Honda. This was the first of many factors that set those women to develop critical animosity toward me. Right away they resented that car—forest green metallic with a slight tinge of blue-green in it, four-door, automatic, but a DX.

Prior to selecting it, I had a dream that I was in an auto underwater and could not open the windows, so I definitely avoided automatic windows and doors. There were times I was very grateful that the DX had been available, also for a lower price than other models. This auto, built in Canada, had an excellent reputation for reliability and performance. The torque was fantastic. It saved my life a few times.

Jeanette fed on their fury by revealing to them that my pay was more than theirs per year, even though all of them, other than Jeannette, had been there longer than I had been. My pay—which was base and $5 for each appointment I made, plus 5 percent of any contract rate signed—was a whopping $25,000 per year.

As marketing coordinator I made over one hundred dials per day, acquired information, and established an understanding of the internal decision-making process within the organizations I dealt with. I engaged in some great conversations with decision makers or anybody willing to talk with me. *The Wall Street Journal*, loaned to me by the comptroller, was my major frame of reference for initiating topics of discussion. For results, I confirmed the expiration date and vendor of their three-to-six-year contracts and made thirty-seven to fifty-five appointments per week for thirteen account executives and five terminal managers in Oregon, Washington, and, at times, British Columbia.

I was an essential support mechanism in the sales effort, mostly the effort for new business. During the entire time I was there, we always surpassed quota. My wonderful boss, Frank, the group manager for Oregon and Washington, said more than once, "Clancy, you continually raise the bar."

Actually, I also helped out with customer service quotas by, without complaint, making follow-up calls on service to existing customers—for two hours every Monday—at the request of the assistant manager. Remember, I was on a small base-plus-incentive pay structure, so my time and financial return were not entirely on the payroll.

I began to mistrust Jeannette when she shared with me sales manager RonVarny's concern with his automobile's front seat, a Chevrolet fleet issue. She overdramatized Ron's conversations with her. RonVarny, the leader in sales production, was a Clint Eastwood look-alike. I exploited that fact to the hilt when attempting to get an appointment for Ron with any female manager with purchasing power. The managers, in turn, often expressed high interest. It was half in fun, the managers and I admitted, but Varny's looks always seemed to draw, giving me an edge.

Jeannette shared his pain and predicaments with me as if I were a management confidante of hers, which I felt was totally out of line, taking into account her very serious responsibilities. She sought me out and expanded upon his case on several occasions: Ron was experiencing great pain and was considering several options, since he was becoming quite desperate. She excused his efforts as just his "getting old, probably arthritis." The first thing he wanted was to have the car's front seat replaced with a customized chair. Then he began to toy with early retirement due to the disability and multiplied by the pain, which he feared would deter him from fulfilling his intended job function.

Jeannette related these to me freely and with a degree of amusement. Ron was not only the sales manager but "top producer." He and I had successfully blitzed the auto agencies in Vancouver, his home, all the way to Olympia and south to Salem and Medford, where we signed up majors, as well as minors. He was phenomenal. I felt awful for his pain and suspected that it could have been brought about by a combination of chemicals and/ or electronics superimposed into his vehicle. Who was out to get him? Who was out to get the company? That was my first hypothesis, an explanation I did not share with Jeannette. She considered herself a first-rate psychologist and often reiterated that she had "a bachelor's in psych." She was very critical, even hypersensitive, of anything off the wall or out of the norm.

Jeannette's amusement infuriated me, and the fact that she freely shared the details with me, not management. Obviously, her first concern was not the major players, and she was devoid of consideration of the potential effect on the sales effort. This was just the start of my severe critique of Jeannette Stork, whose credentials mostly relied on the fact that she was the wife of a policeman, albeit the second wife.

She also shared with me her experiences with her husband's first wife. Her assessment of his ex-wife was mostly an evaluation of that person's weight, which was greater than Jeannette's. "I'm only sixty pounds overweight because my husband insists on barbecue, mostly steaks, every night. My sex life is superb," she further insisted. She collected artwork, the several irises by Georgia O'Keefe, which inspired her further into the "intricacies of the vagina."

My response to a discussion of two events, one in the city and one in the accounting department—responses contrary to those of the other women—further redefined my status. Jeannette's husband was with the city's SWAT team. He was a former military MP, "a valued marksman," she often reminded anyone in earshot. It served to support her claims of the need to verify the working status of immigrant labor. There was shortly a police sweep of immigrant labor at the company. Jeannette was forewarned and readily passed the test. No undocumented employees were found in the plant. This recognition made her even more aggressive.

CHAPTER FOUR

The Sting?

Then came, I swear, a set-up, a sting-like operation.

The accounting clerks immediately rejected the introduction of Sebastian Le Clerq, a college graduate in accounting, as the comptroller's accounting assistant, who was to oversee their department in the absence of the comptroller. The girls (women) didn't like him. He was an American Indian from Klamath Falls, unsophisticated and surely not up to their million-dollar-plus billing per week. He was hired by corporate merely to meet the minority quota stipulations, the girls felt, and they vented their resentment by letting Jeannette know she better do something about it, especially via *her* connections with corporate.

The large window in Jeannette's office, which had been the prior accounting assistant's office, looked out on the girls' desks. They had easy access to her, day in, day out. Or rather, she enjoyed dominant oversight of them. Sebastian was merely given one of the vacant Steelcase desks. They all gave him the cold shoulder. For Sebastian, this was a big-time corporation, his opportunity for a real career to fulfill his dreams, as he was just out of college though in his thirties. He had served in the military out of high school before attending college, and with a family in tow, it had taken more than four years to finish his degree.

Suddenly, a new customer service assistant was hired. She was a knock-out looker and sweet and friendly. She welcomed his conversation first thing in the morning, before the phones opened. She was a godsend to Sebastian because he had no one else to talk with. Her costume led me to suspect all was not normal or ordinary. This was 1996, before the introduction of the

V-neck revealing lots of cleavage. This was before the "Revolution of 2005 when the bulge of breasts and bare throats all of a sudden burst on the horizon, commanding one's entire, somewhat uncomfortable, attention.

This lady with arched brows, false eyelashes, color-alive makeup, and all smiles was adorned by sheer prints, which were out of season and just a little too obvious, revealing big boobs-a-bouncing, like out of Victoria's Secret. Sebastian found his way down the hall from the large accounting space to the smaller customer service phone room and spent the first half hour of each morning charmed by and enamored with her. I never knew her name.

Then one Monday morning, Jeannette notified me of a meeting at ten o'clock for "accounting *and* marketing" in the coffee room.

"The new customer service assistant has given notice," Jeannette announced. "She gave me the note given to her by Sebastian, which was so embarrassing and humiliating that she has quit and will not return to work under any circumstance."

Jeannette did not show us the note, nor did she read it to us. And suddenly I realized that Sebastian was not at this meeting. Neither was the comptroller.

"It's too suggestive," Jeannette said of the note, "uses really unmentionable…er…well! I want you to vote to remove Sebastian from employment."

Immediately, I smelled a rat. This lady—so insulted, supposedly so embarrassed, so humiliated, in her early thirties—had to be a decoy, a set-up. Jeannette must have used her police connections to bring in a pro to royally set up this poor sap, the unsuspecting Sebastian.

On the other hand, her accounting clerks, the women, were outraged by his so-called "note." "Sebastian's married" and "He has two children," they uttered again and again. "He's got a problem." "He just caused us to lose a valuable new employee." "What's wrong with him?" "He's just a sex pervert, nothing else!" They all voted to fire him.

I objected, to no avail. On my side, the so-called customer service vacancy left by the "actress" was never again recruited for or filled! Why not? The evidence indicated that there never was any customer service opening. It had been merely devised to get rid of one strongly opposed accounting assistant, Sebastian Le Clerq.

This was at least my third confrontation or run-in with the accounting, payroll, billing, and now human resources crew. Two or three months earlier, a kid just fired by United Parcel Service (the brown shirts) had attempted to reach the sixth floor of the KOIN building in downtown Portland with a rifle because one of the clerks on that floor had openly made fun of him. He'd been new on the job, and he felt she had caused him to be fired.

The clerks had all ganged up on the kid with a gun. I'd merely tried to point out that if we treat people badly, we cause them undue harm. Our treatment triggers "acting out" on their part, and we should be held partly responsible. The gay violinist at Rutgers who committed suicide in 2010 as a result of bullying illustrates my point. The two students who filmed his sexual encounters and exploited them on the Internet have been removed from the college, for a start.

Anyway, the clerks, outraged at my point of view, overreacted. They were very eager to point out what a complete loser the UPS kid was, "probably his entire life." Why else would the office clerk "criticize" the kid in the "ill-fitting all-brown uniform. Of course, he wasn't doing his job." They were all right. He was all wrong. "He should be behind bars, kept away from normal folk," they said.

Then another controversial incident occurred. Jeanette's husband was in the news. Called by a small mental hospital via 911, he'd shot to death an unarmed Hispanic who'd been taken to one of the mental wards. The man was trying to get out, and hospital personnel couldn't restrain him.

To complicate matters, no one had spoken to the man in Spanish, his language. Hell, he probably didn't know what was going on. Jeannette, naturally, and the women, of course, defended her husband. I didn't criticize this time or even offer options or alternatives, but I sure did ask lots of questions. That didn't set right with the girls, which was apparent as they tried to defend and explain and went out on limbs of "what if" when none of us really had enough information regarding the situation.

Later on, that hospital was shut down for good. Yeah!

CHAPTER FIVE

Teeth

F rank personally told me that five years with the company now entitled me to Amegal group dental insurance. I had dire reason to take advantage of that immediately. The only problem was that dentists on the list in my adjacent zip codes were not taking additional patients. After a degree of effort, I finally connected with a Dr. Goen—of Chinese descent and a recent graduate of the University of Oregon Dental School—in a new office on SE 122nd Avenue.

The office complex was part of a series of one-story duplexes built for professional services, with lots of off-street parking and handsome landscaping: flowering cherry trees, junipers, mature rhododendrons and camellias, and ground cover of clipped and controlled ivy that revealed ordered cement walkways. It was an area, though, that suffered turnover of the professionals, maybe because it was situated—regardless of how attractive and professional-looking– in a low-income zip code, according to political statisticians. It attracted the disabled, working poor, and, especially, new immigrants from the numerous low-rent apartments.

I consulted with my regular dentist, who shared a building with his wife, a travel agent who specialized in tours to the Middle East. "I find the Arab men very attractive," Wanda had said more than once. She and Ron Nakata, a second-generation Japanese man, met when they were in training for the CIA. They saved their money and returned to Portland to go to dental school after they left the CIA. They were good friends of my brother and had designed my upper dentures, which required a special overbite because I was born with an underbite that required orthodontics when I was ten to twelve.

Dr. Nakata did a beautiful job. Now he said to go ahead and use the group dentist but warned, "You will be back."

"Why do you say that?" I asked.

"I just know you will be back," the dear dentist surmised.

Dr. Goen was going to fill a cavity in a right molar. Her assistant, also a doctor, used a syringe with a long needle and hit a nerve on my upper jaw. Very shortly I felt like I had been hit with something like amphetamines, as they have been described to me. I was totally jazzed up, and I knew my heartbeat was going bonkers. Moreover, I was angry. There is a drug out there that makes one angry and, I swear, can cause a heart attack because it causes one to roil and roil. At the same time, the good Dr. Goen insisted that she could not attend to my dental needs until I subjected myself to a periodontist, but she couldn't recommend one. Strange, there was no apparent reason for that shot and no follow-up procedure.

I took this request for a periodontist very seriously and even consulted with Dr. Nakata regarding Dr. Goen's insistence on a specialist. He said she knew what she was talking about.

The dental group listed no periodontists in my area. I found a questionable one. I admit I had reservations but ventured forth. It was a small office in a large "professional" complex. There were straps on the arms of the chair. There was the nurse and the dentist. I sank into the chair. While the dentist (who looked like my awful neighbor's brother-in-law who earlier had pretended to be a telephone company employee when I had had trouble with my phone) prepared a long needle, the nurse started to draw the straps across my arms.

I jumped out of the chair and hollered, "Forget it! Let me out of here." I ran out to my auto, frantically started it, and found the freeway, getting as far away from there as I could. Later, I went back to check that office and it was, of course, empty.

A dear friend had told me that when he'd been in Washington, DC, for an internship, he'd gone to a dentist like this who put a long needle into the roof of his mouth. It knocked him out. When he woke up, all evidence of the dentist had been removed from the two-room office rental, and all of his hair fell out at the roots. Fortunately, the straps had been removed as well. How macabre.

I still had pain in the molar, and it seemed that the best thing to do was to adhere to Dr. Goen's requirement that I visit a periodontist.

Dr. Fromm wanted payment in cash. The group dental didn't cover periodontics. His large office in a Vancouver medical/dental complex off I-205 sported photos on the left wall of the entry, most of South American youths with cleft-palate-like conditions before and normal mouths and smiles after. While applying lots of Novocain, he asked several questions, the first of which was how I found Dr. Goen.

"What do you see in Orientals anyway? What's wrong with us white guys?" he asked. "I understand you garden," he went on. "So do I, but my wife now has my garden. She's divorcing me."

Still without any response from me, his hand in my mouth with the syringe, he went on. "You said your favorite is roses; you have thirty-seven? I had forty-eight geraniums. I love geraniums. My wife doesn't garden."

He said all this in a somewhat matter-of-fact but sardonic, bitter tone, a cover-up for intense anger. At me? Like he knew I was recently divorced and, of course, like his wife, I had taken some poor sap to the cleaners, which was not the case. At the least, I felt foreboding. I really asked myself, *Is this guy stable?*

Dr. Fromm took a razor with a long handle, like that of a barber's in movies about godfathers, and merely sliced it down between each tooth, all the teeth—even the healthy front ones, *the smile ones, which were in perfect alignment*—so that when they healed and fortunately did not fall out they'd be lifted up from their root base, taller by an eighth to a quarter inch and tumbling over each other like leaning, tall pillars. I knew he was cutting the nerves to the bone. He did quickly suture the back molars and gave me a prescription for a pain-killer. My son would pick me up after surgery, so I read my *Time* and waited the half hour required in the inner reception area.

We got the prescription filled before going home. My regular pharmacist at Menlo Park warned me that the opiate was a very powerful one, so he broke it in half for me. "This half will knock a hundred-and-fifty-pound person out; take only when necessary."

Once home, I bit a quarter-inch edge off the awful chalky thing and prepared for the worst. The teeth were all loose. I began to pray that they didn't fall out, which I realize now they were supposed to. And I thanked the Lord that the pain was not as bad as it should have been under the circumstances. I felt fortunate that I could avoid taking any more pain-killer.

Fortunately, it was only the bottom teeth. For the top I used dentures, which were beautiful and an authentic color. Strangely enough, Dr. Goen recoiled when she saw my teeth. I spoke angrily to her about it. She was already unhappy with me because earlier I had told her I would accept only her dentistry in her office, no one else's. Next, she sent me a letter saying I had been rude to her staff, she was returning my check, and she could no longer attend to me.

I was surely confused by all this. In my mind I overdramatized it to the extreme, if that were possible. Why? Was I actually being punished for something? Maybe Dr. Goen was Taiwanese and one of those – anti-mainland China?

I revisited Dr. Nakata, and he sawed down the jagged front bottom teeth to return my smile and chewing bite. But he would give no opinion of the so-called surgery. Professional people, unless their careers depend on it, avoid testifying in court about their fellows.

I deeply suspected that the photographs of mostly brown, disfigured children were after Dr. Fromm had worked them over. His cold nurse (she didn't look at me, wasn't cheery, and was rather mechanical) merely said when I had inquired of the photos, "The doctor doesn't do that anymore."

Since it seemed to me that the actual roots of my teeth were dislodged and possibly relocated, I began to have a lingering, recurring fear that my identity by dental X-ray had actually been altered.

That's preposterous, Clancy, I tell myself. *But the farfetched is ever possible. People have access to tidbits of information, true or false, up the wazoo – these days.*

CHAPTER SIX
Kind of Odd

When I filled up the gas tank of my new auto that I kept in my garage, I had evidence that someone was able to access it. I kept mileage mostly to find out the miles-per-gallon performance. From time to time, there was an extra fifty to seventy-five miles on it, clocked overnight, I thought, but the car could have been used while I thought it was parked on the street during work.

I had reason not to trust my neighbors next door. They were really friends of Brad, had sworn allegiance to my ex-husband (yeah, one of those) and for years knew where the extra key to the house was kept. Plus, I had reason to believe they'd even interrupted my mail, which was not keyed down but merely in a big mail box on the curb anybody could access.

Then, all of a sudden, some insulation was exposed on my dashboard, which led me to believe that someone had removed the unit, possibly used the space among the wires in which to put contraband (drugs, of course), then screwed the dash down again. How else could a slight swath of cotton-like insulation squeeze out? I took the car to the company fleet mechanic and explained to him my suspicions. I asked him if he could remove the dashboard and check for me.

"I'd go directly to the police," I said, "but I don't have enough evidence, just the mileage, not closely tracked, and this exposed cotton stuff. It wasn't there before."

The mechanic acted scared. "Well, if I have time. Is it authorized?"

"I would have Frank's go-ahead," I assured him. "He would feel there's cause. But he's in Denver, and I don't bother him there. I could ask Ron

Varny, but he's on a short leave of absence. Besides, I report directly to Frank, just like Jeannette does. This is not priority. I'm just asking you to do it when you have the extra time to do so. It's obvious why it should be done. This could be a police matter," I persuaded further.

He kept saying, "I dunno."

That evening my auto was outside the garage, inside the chain link fence that corralled the entire plant campus, with the keys inside. The cotton-like wad, that twist of insulation, was gone, but Albert, the mechanic, was nowhere in sight. It was several days before I was able to connect with him again.

"Did you find anything?" I asked. "Was there anything? Had it been used for something?"

He just muttered, "Talk to Jeannette" and turned away from me.

At about that same time, two telephone people spent a week behind my wall, in the hallway, on the phone system. Shortly after, I had to dial almost twenty times to get beyond a busy tone. My reports on the fax to my people (all nineteen of them, including Frank) at 6:30 a.m. now took until 9:00 a.m. to transmit.

In fact, the area code to Tacoma—where we had a new salesman who seemed to brag, claiming military connections—switched over to an area code in Michigan. I reported this odd phenomenon to none other than the comptroller himself and also included the time delays on the fax. He merely said, "You put too much information on the page, so it takes much longer to transmit."

The number of characters has nothing to do with the speed of trans-mission. Why did he say such a thing? Quite a talker, the salesman out of Tacoma "swore by TPC," which I assumed was an automotive additive. TPC was later identified to me as an acronym for a highly questionable organiza-tion, Total Population Control.

This situation was instigated because the staff wanted me to move to the new plant. But no one told me that my sales crew wanted me to join them at their offices. In a short while, Jeannette merely told Frank that I "refused" to move. Further, she said that I had told her that Frank had "sexually harassed" me and I intended to make a case of it. How ludicrous. I had once told Frank that in my long career "I have never been sexually harassed."

He'd laughed and said, "You probably were and didn't know it."

I loved that retort. My boss and I had something special, which Jeannette intruded upon and attempted to destroy.

Frank and I talked sports and family, mostly. His only son was terribly short for team sports, so Frank was encouraging him to consider wrestling. My boss hauled the local Little League team—which he coached and which included his son, a second baseman— to practice and games in his company Suburban.

One of his grandfathers was a minister in Detroit, then Denver. Denver was home. His other grandfather was a miner and a union man. With that information he and I agreed with his grandfather: If business goes down, "don't lay me off, instead reduce my wages." I shared a book I was reading by Paul Krugman, a Nobel-winning American economist who pointed out that GDP growth rate was only 2.5 percent, yet companies were insisting on 10 percent increases in sales production quotas year after year and imposing lots of pressure on personnel to make it happen. We were mutually concerned.

CHAPTER SEVEN
The Pink Slip

The company hired a new CEO, female, who was riding high due to her recent coup. She had been given credit for acquiring the IN/OUT Delivery's infamous contract with a quasifederal agency. It necessitated IN/OUT to multiply their Boeing 747 fleet numerous times to fulfill the all-encompassing international contract. She was selected to take our privately held firm public on the New York Stock Exchange.

The Oregon/Washington group first got wind of her when her personal staffer, supposedly a sales management expert, arrived in town and instantly fired our sales manager while Frank was in Denver.

Frank was in Denver because the company had purchased a high-end exclusive design and manufacturing company located in that city. Corporate wanted to pay pattern cutters and power sewers the same wages paid to inventory and washer attendants in the other units of the company. The new Denver outfit balked at that, so their administrators walked off the job. Frank was required to troubleshoot the situation and hire new administrators to impose the new owner's policy. In other words, to see that corporate won out.

Yes, things were getting heavy-handed. All of a sudden the company was imposing central control against any local autonomy that had been allowed to develop over the years. Local units had been allowed to respond to unique situations in a given area. For example, our group had altered teams to more closely service our giant accounts such as Boeing, Weyerhaeuser, Les Schwab, Wacker Siltronic, and TriMet. I had been responsible for bringing in these last two firms and increasing business at new outlets of the other three. I had established a working relationship with many Boeing contractors in

Kent, Washington, and was getting close to opening the door to Precision Castparts, Northwest Natural Gas, and General Telephone (GTE).

At the same time, men in the field told me about their encounters with the representative sent out by the incoming CEO. Mostly, their reaction was to throw in the towel. One fellow, in Washington for sixteen years, was seriously toying with the notion of returning home. "I guess I'll go back to the old homestead in Pennsylvania and try farming again," he muttered over the phone to me after an extensive description of his confrontation with the new CEO's mascot.

On January 31· 1998, Jeanette called me into the office. Frank was there with tears in his eyes. Jeannette told me without fanfare that I was terminated as of that day. The comptroller said that my department was being closed and returned to the marketing effort in Burbank, western corporate headquarters, where all other group marketing had been traditionally located. Later on that same day, in his office, the comptroller offered me $3,500 severance pay if I would sign a pledge that I would bring no legal grievances against the company. I turned him down and gave it no more thought.

By July unemployment had run out, and with no job offers and no income, I applied to retrieve my 401K. I was told by Jeanette that it was in moratorium and unavailable. I claimed an exception of hardship. Jeanette did not process it and was unavailable to see me. Nine months later I received my 401K, now at $21,000, just half its value at the date of termination. At sixty-one, though with no job prospects yet, I had at least ten years of productivity left in me.

The CEO lasted less than two years. She did take the company public. Ultimately, the principals bought out their shares on the NYSE and returned control to their private hands. In her sweep, despite our consistent profitable operation, all fourteen personnel in our group lost their jobs, including my dear group manager, Frank Clausen, just one year after my release. In 1998 we suffered what happened to too many people in 2008.

So I did apply prematurely for social security. The reality of that made a great impact on me since I would lose immediately six hundred dollars per month. It had taken me ten years and a master's degree to earn the same amount I had as a stewardess right out of college with Pan American World

CHAPTER EIGHT
Initial Stab at It

My first inclination was to try to save my house by continuing to work any job I could find at $8 an hour and get additional income by renting out my wonderful master bedroom with adjoining bath. Across the street, when the man divorced his wife, the mother of his two teenage children, she resorted to renting one of her four bedrooms to a student at the chiropractic college nearby.

A social worker with the state called regarding my advertisement for the room in *The Oregonian* . She brought Vincenzio, a wiry, lively black man, with her to view the facility. He had just been awarded custody of his two sons, eight and ten, and was employed as a "chemist," he said, at the Styrofoam plant not too far east of my home. Later, by his description, I came to understand that he used a patented formula, added ingredients like a cook or paint mixer would, and—voila!—produced loads of Styrofoam, which was then cut to size by others for sale, packaging, and shipment. The social worker paid me $500 for his first month's rent, but Vincenzio would pay the rent from then on, she explained.

I slept in my son's room, on the sofa in my den with the computer, and sometimes on the nine-foot sofa, which was really comfortable, in the family room with television.

Vincenzio—Vin, for short—loved to cook and made apparently healthy food (lots of fried meat but with fresh veggies) for the two boys. On paydays he did a huge shopping at WinCo. My small, U-shaped kitchen was short of storage, but there was plenty of storage in the garage, adjacent to the family room, that opened to the kitchen. The youngsters spent all their nonschool time (they were attending summer school) in their room, watching TV and listening to music. They understandably didn't seem comfortable with me, but they briefly mentioned their maternal grandparents who were white and, fortunately, visited with them on weekends.

Vin was quirky. By the third day, he asked me, "Don't you do sex?"

I immediately retorted, "Absolutely not."

He said, "I've always done it with whoever I'm living with."

"Forget it," I told him. "I'm not a candidate."

This was midsummer. That first hot Saturday afternoon, he sported a green-and-white Hawaiian-motifed pair of shorts, which happened to be mine. I had to argue with him to change out of them into his own clothes so I could retrieve my shorts. Then my favorite CDs—like Credence Clearwater Revival and the one with "Louie Louie" by the Kingsmen—began disappearing. Apparently, he had taken possession.

Shortly after that he talked of a "wow" girl he had met and was seeing, "a vice president of the company next door." He passionately described her looks and his feelings for her. After only a few weeks had gone by, when doing my usual yard work, I found beer bottles outside the windows of the boarders' room, in the blue hydrangeas bed. *Such trashy treatment*, I thought. *Why there? It made me suspicious, to say the least.*

So later that night—it was a Wednesday—I knocked on the door at about eight o'clock and finally talked the boys into opening it. I didn't feel I should just enter unannounced. Vincenzio was nowhere in the room. The window was wide open on the west end of the wall, and its screen was nowhere in sight. Plain and simple, Vin was leaving the house via the window for, apparently, a rendezvous with his girlfriend, leaving his boys alone.

I reported this immediately to the social worker, on her voice mail because, naturally, she never answered her phone. Vin wanted me to think he was on the premises, in the room with his boys. How terrible. *I can't be responsible for this*, I thought. I became terribly afraid and terribly angry. I felt so bad for his sons. Moreover, I feared the responsibility of being, unknowingly, the only adult in the household—their caretaker, so to speak. God save me.

I left their door open and stayed up for Vincenzio's return. About 3:00 a.m. he crawled back in through the same window, and I presented him with a written notice. I told him I would testify against him in court if he wasn't out by the weekend.

Shortly thereafter I put my dream house up for sale. It took longer to sell because the realtor, it turned out, was not available on weekends. He had to go to church and entertain his eight-year-old daughter from a former marriage. I found out later that he advertised my house only on the Internet; at that time, 1999, the Internet was not widely accessed by the larger market for real estate purposes. The newspapers still predominated for real estate information. His agency didn't spend one dime to promote my home but insisted that they featured it as "an executive find" on the Internet, due to its location, I guess, in proximity to the airport. "Fit for an executive" was very misleading. There were many homes like it at the time, with beamed vaulted ceilings and hardwood floors. Selling points, I thought, were the garden and the huge covered front porch, plus the white brick fireplace was like new, having never had a fire in it. No wonder most people passed over it.

The only offer I got for the house was from a couple I later found out attended the realtor's same church. How does that sit pretty! When they took over the keys, the wife mentioned that her husband was a postal employee at the main Portland office. She actually admitted awaiting a disability determination due to a bad back as a former employee with Fred Meyer. The couple had just sold their double-wide trailer home in Wilsonville. They had no children, and it sounded like their intention was to shortly resell. To boot, they had to order a reduced-sized refrigerator. The huge one that was delivered didn't fit into its designation in the kitchen, which, I admit, tickled me.

I reported these discrepancies to the real estate investigative agency of the state of Oregon. A young female investigator, just out of college, found nothing out of order.

Whereas my job at the company, plus my part-time job of twenty additional hours per week for a total of sixty hours per week, had paid all the bills with something left over, I was now working part-time only for $8 to $10 an hour and squeaking by with help from my son and brother to keep up the house payments, operate the auto, and eat. The $500 rent payment would make up the difference, but the risks were so great. Clearing the cuttings from grass and the extra-large yard with twenty-three blue hydrangeas and thirty-seven rose bushes, plus weeds from a wild north forty, cost me $400 each of three times during the growing season for a Dumpster. Just prior to the divorce, my ex-husband had offered the oversized garage for three Kiwanis garage-sale fund-raisers. He left the rejects, mostly junk such as torn t-shirts, soiled items, odd cookware, strange tools, camping gear, broken toys, which I disposed of via many trips to the Goodwill in my auto.

This gives me a chance to soapbox. If I have something that now qualifies for second-hand, something that I no longer value or want to keep, I do not put a price tag on it for tax-deduction purposes or for resale. Since it is no longer valuable to me, I give it away free, gratis, at a zero evaluation, although a math professor friend of mine once said, "Zero holds, represents, a value as well. It is, after all, a digit. It occupies valuable space, so it is a number."

CHAPTER NINE

A Fun Gold Mine

A good thing came out of that real estate firm. When it happened, the sale of my home was so sudden that their choice of a condo for me to purchase was an option I dared not pass up. After paying my debt to my son and brother and splitting with my ex-husband, I put the remaining proceeds into my future home to keep the mortgage payments low. The owner had made alterations that would prove to be very valuable, ultimately contributing to the beauty and function of the place.

For one, he had invested in an Amana washer and dryer that he'd left in place. Indestructible. In the entry and kitchen, he had installed sturdy 13" x 13" stone floor tile, rust and dark blue-green. In the stairwell he'd installed beams to define the staircase, making it truly open, and he'd bored a thirty-six-inch-high hole in the kitchen wall, finished and framed, that further opened horizontally along the lines of the upper staircase. It let in light from the two-story window on the stair landing so that the alley of the kitchen enjoyed western sunlight in the afternoon. Morning sun came in through the dining room at the east end of the kitchen. The dining area's wide windows looked out on a vacant lot beyond the fence, where firs stood and five plum trees bloomed in the spring.

The previous owner had made makeshift cabinets in the pantry, with space for a very small microwave at the top, and put a huge fridge in the tallest space under the stairwell. I quickly removed the refrigerator, which was an energy sucker, and tore out the shelves. It opened up the pantry for storage purposes—potatoes, garlic, spices, sugar, flour, nuts, beans, and pasta. Eventually I had a handyman finish it uniform with the stair beams, with two-by-sixes. I painted it all with white oil-based enamel. Later on a handyman built a custom thirteen-shelf cabinet against the inside wall of the pantry for canned goods to free up my lower cabinet space. On the back wall of the staircase in the pantry, I installed my blue-green-and-white plaid wallpaper, left over from my old kitchen.

It is not "executive-level" finishing. It definitely retains a do-it-yourself look. The previous owner had also placed 6" x 6" oak squares parquet style on the living and dining room floors. They were rough on the edges. Over the next ten years, I was able to get O'Malley's Family Floors, just relocated from San Francisco, to sand, fill with wood putty, then polyurethane the flooring after it was vandalized in 2003. The damage included the destruction of the molding and front door framing when the vandals tore it down January 18, 2003. Unemployed from 2002 to 2004, I did police volunteer work and reported mostly crimes against businesses. Someone must have had me on his or her radar, which might explain the vandalism.

The previous owner had taken the doors off the kitchen cabinets for open, easy-to-access cupboards. He anchored navy-blue-and-white six-inch tiles in one row across the backsplash and on the high, island-like counter that divided the living room from the kitchen. Someone had replaced his top-of-the-line chef's range with one that was ready for recycling, so I had to buy a new range, a more economical one.

The vandals, in 2003, tore out the indirect lighting in the kitchen; soaked artwork in water; destroyed the computer, monitor, printer, and dishwasher; tore out electrical outlets; cracked and chipped sinks in the bathrooms; and poured water on the wood floor, the parquet, which swelled some of the squares, dislodging them. After I found a job with income in 2004, Portland Development Commission loaned me $5,000 to replace damaged plumbing and lighting, install electrical units, repair the flooring, and replace the front door. My homeowner's insurance wouldn't pay it because the company reported I was engaged in a "high-risk occupation" and hadn't informed them of such, so I should have been in a different insurance category.

I got a great boost to my budget when I sold my Honda in 2004 and selected TriMet for a monthly bus pass, still under $30. When I was a police volunteer, I filled the gas tank up for $10 almost daily. The IRS recognized my unofficial volunteer status expenditures, but without income other than social security, it barely reimbursed.

Giving up my auto was one of the most difficult things I have ever had to do. In the summer on weekends, I'd love to drive north on I-5, cross the bridge across the Columbia at Longview to Rainier, and return on Highway 30 with my windows wide open, my radio on full blast with classical to jazz. Or I'd drive east on the Washington side, taking Highway 14 to the Bridge of the Gods at Hood River and return on I-84 to Portland.

Sometimes I even did this on streets south of my home that I had never been on before to look for gardens and architecture, even people. Since they would wave from their perches on the front steps of their mostly modest homes in the early evening, you could tell they still took pride in possession. Their daily labor paid for their homes and the local school for their children.

On one of those trips on a Sunday in mid-March 2002, I saw an unscheduled single-engine plane land at an *abandoned WWI airfield* in Kelso, Washington. Immediately, tremendous intrusion occurred in my home, phone, and job due to my effort to merely report it to authorities. In June 2002 I participated in curtailing a gathering for a planned rumble against a black race-car driver with North Carolina license plates. At five o'clock on a Saturday morning, he had a gorgeous apple-red race car in tow behind a white, late model Ford 350 pickup in the parking lot of an athletic club with national membership.

In July, the phone repairman told me that there was a brass unit inserted on my GE phone, on a landline, sending my calls to a phone bank with a reverse ID that merely pretended to be whoever I was calling. Further, he said, there was a phone "out of our system," programmed to dial my number over and over again – blocking any calls but with the capacity to pick up my voice mail. He said my only choice was to cancel my service.

Among other things, I reported an arson set up against Wizer's market in Lake Oswego, possibly instigated by delivery of green lumber to a construction site next door. I fell into several other crimes while looking for work and reported them first to the companies involved. They then decided what to do as far as police were concerned. One event included an inside job I reported to the general manager of a large food distribution company in Wilsonville.

He fired his sales manager, who had tried to circumvent me from reporting it, and hired two additional inventory workers. The incident involved the company's charitable donations to nonprofit organizations being siphoned off by truckers in unmarked rental vehicles.

At 6:00 p.m. one day, I walked in on a phony company that was using my job prospect's facility, warehouse, and trucks for its own operation after hours. When I returned to talk to the pipe company's general manager, who had my resume for a position in inside sales, he said, "Clancy, I am exceedingly grateful to you. You're overqualified for any job I have."

Before I sold my Honda in 2004, it was stolen in August 2002, so I was introduced to travel by bus. The auto was recovered in September. My home was vandalized on January 18, 2003. When I refinanced my condo in 2006, the police notified the bank of identity theft because they'd found that two driver's licenses in my name, but with another's photo, had been used by someone else.

From October 2004 to July 2006, I worked in customer service at Sprint/ Nextel, over sixty-five hours per week (burnout hours). The $27,000 a year helped me pay back Portland Development Commission, put 13" x 13" Italian ceramic tile (in multiple shades of blue and purple) on the main hallway, bathroom, and utility floors, and Armstrong black walnut laminate in the den, which looks south onto my walled garden.

I also installed 18" x 18" American Olean textured tile, a pattern called Ocean, in the two-room bathroom off the large bedroom upstairs. My last projects included a handsome 26" x 21" overhead range hood in white metal. I refinished the indirect lighting and covered it with cut stained-glass squares of textured, burnished gold and dark green over the island counter between the living room and kitchen.

When I'd first moved in, I invited my old supervisor from the high school, Norm Kuhlman, and his new wife, Lorraine, for lunch. They had joined forces after losing their first spouses, bought a house together, and shared their love of gardening. They especially loved roses. I had moved many of my roses from my old house into pots and brought them to my garden space here at the condo. But they were suffering from not enough sun, due to the obstruction of a giant plum tree in front of the garden wall.

The couple expressed concern for my roses' survival without enough sunlight. Without telling me, Normand Lorraine contacted the homeowners association of our thirty condos and offered to pay for the removal of the plum tree because, they said, it disrupted the cement curb and, ultimately, the storm pipe drainage system. The home owners board took them up on it. Thanks to the Kuhlmans my garden now has lots of sun. I wasn't told of their efforts on my behalf until several years later.

For my birthday in June 2005, I bought one hundred shares of General Electric at $37 each. In 2008 they went down to $5 and now sit at $27. My grunt job also financed my photo project, *Flowers in Felony Flats*, ninety-nine pages featuring people I'd met on the bus at 5:50 a.m., at work, and in my neighborhood. I took it to my fiftieth high school reunion. Photos of my garden took up the last half of the book. I think of people as flowers too.

When unemployed, between jobs, I didn't have enough income to sustain myself. My mother used to say, "Live on the income you are able to generate and save some of that as well. Don't dip into your rainy day savings." So I resorted, reluctantly, to renting out my big bedroom with private bath, which included kitchen access, washer/dryer, cable, and off-street parking. Many have informed me that my rental is first-rate, an exceptional value.

If sometimes my report sounds like a financial ledger, that's life, isn't it? Unlike most stories, especially fiction, people seem to live lives apart from any so-called money. They're just poor or rich or nouveau riche or independently wealthy. I do not classify myself on the socioeconomic scale, although I qualify as low-income even when there is a rent payment to report. I tend to lean toward economic determinism and remain a fan of Maslow. That is, basic needs have to be met before self-realization can occur.

CHAPTER TEN

Last Try

I've found that my story is happening to lots of people in their fifties, especially since 2008—an individual finds his or her job ending prematurely, is not of a mind-set or financially capable of retirement, and still wants the vigorous and challenging lifestyle of the employed; especially since they are in possession of the energy, preparation and experience to do so.

I was lucky. It happened to me before so many doors of opportunity were shut by the downturn in the economy—the deflation of property values, in particular. Yet it took me quite some time to recognize the signs. I would not have left Sprint/Nextel, no matter how gruesome that position, if in 2006 I had known there would be no other job opportunity ever for me. I continued to apply vigorously for work until November 2011, when I made my last effort to apply at OMSI, Oregon Museum of Science and Industry, for a researcher and writer position.

In my cover letter, I made an all-out effort to illustrate my credentials for research and up-to-date know-how:

> Currently, I am mostly dependent on what I read to update my knowledge of scientific innovation. When I was a police volunteer (2002–2004), I did observe that the juxtaposition of inanimate objects can create energy, and that laser units can remove all fluids from an auto and its auxiliary equipment. Intermittent and unpredictable, nonrhythmic sound blasts can interrupt electronic transmissions.
>
> A handheld auto demolition tool can enter the human body without tearing it and can tunnel and burst where it is programmed

to cause damage. It leaves the metal surface unscathed or the flesh bruised by the force of its entry, but does not tear it.

Chemical vapors, including cyanide, and possibly isotopes can be transmitted via radio waves to a target. The walkie-talkie manufactured by Motorola has been used for such purposes. These have all been confirmed by Robert J. Oppenheimer's theorems of the early 1930s, described in *The American Prometheus*, a biography of the physicist made famous by his team's development of the atomic bomb.

Recent science articles in the *Economist* that I sent on to my grandchildren follow in shortened version:

American ships are loaded down with the metal (copper) required for communications, including sonar. Now it has been demonstrated that lightweight plastic tubes filled with seawater (salt?) can transmit same. In fact, they work even filled with Gatorade (sugar?). Still, we need copper to resist electronic intrusion.

Another article of potentially great significance is titled "Printing of Batteries." A Florida company can print the chemical components of batteries on paper inexpensively, possibly eliminating the necessity to encase the action.

I was so lucky to rent my room, but it is a precarious undertaking, many times heart-wrenching, sometimes an everyday torturous human drama that only the brave in heart or the hungry can undertake. In these pages, a very awful human drama unfolds. It is painful to relate, dredge up, recall. At times I have called it a war zone. I can see each of my renters vividly, feel in my gut their very—yes—tragic existences. This is not a celebration. It is merely a raw revelation of the struggles of humanity, of human foibles, frailty, and even some tiny triumphs—always to someone else's disadvantage. Nobody gains. A high price is paid for business as usual. What some people won't do for money! Or what people *have* to do for money. My mother used to say, "I don't *have* to do anything but die and pay taxes."

CHAPTER ELEVEN
The Train in the Night

I didn't make the transition from my home of thirty years to a condo gracefully, although looking back, I did accept the facts at hand without tears, but with a lot of fear. I arranged with a transfer company to deliver my son's possessions to his family home in Tigard and my ex-husband's to his retirement facility at the edge of Tualatin. He had found work as a bus driver for a school district. I had always encouraged him to find paid work and give up commissioned sales and suggested school bus driving more than once. At that time he'd considered it beneath him. Finally, he got practical. Friends said the kids absolutely loved him.

In short, the transfer company delivered to my son ten boxes of *Sports Illustrated, Baseball Digest,*, Baseball Digest, , and *Sport*, plus my piano, a standard size spinet. From the family room, I gave him the large dining table that extended to seat eight comfortably with chairs. On it I had cut out Vogue couturier patterns for suits for work and upholstery for the Italian transitional sofa, a project with my friend Maura Dee, mother of my son's best friend, Sean. After his mother died following a ten-year struggle with breast cancer, Sean dropped out of college and lived with us for two years. We held Cub Scout meetings on the table in the 1970s and played lots of penny poker, blackjack, and Trivial Pursuit on it.

On the table I'd also served lots of buffets, including hot hors d'oeuvres like cheddar cheese puffs, stuffed spinach in toasted phyllo, and mushroom crescents made out of cream cheese dough, and a stuffed rosemary turkey and marinated pasta salad for twenty-five women on a Saturday for my fifty-fifth birthday. There were also the rib-eye roasts and smoked turkeys and the BYOL for ninety-nine at the surprise forty-fifth birthday party for my husband in 1979. I'd scrubbed the garage floor and set up the lawn furniture to make enough room for all the guests since it was November and into the rainy season.

Thinking of that night, I could see Theresa Dengh, who brought her almond cookies to the event, Alexander, her husband, and one of their sons peeling giant shrimp for the seven-course feast Alex cooked at least three times in my little kitchen (he brought his own wok) for four couples, all New Ladder agents. Ultimately, Theresa was also hired by Ladder to work with mostly Asian customers whose policies' cash reserves had been spent by a dishonest agent to create and finance more policies to meet sales quotas. She translated for them and administered the reimbursements by the company of their life insurance policies.

Cooking from 3:00 to 6:00 a.m., I'd created bacon, garlic, and asparagus quiche, a giant sirloin roast, and a variety of salads for our son's wedding rehearsal for seventy-five friends in the backyard in July 1991. The kitchen table was also where my husband had done his taxes and written speeches for Toastmasters and Kiwanis.

The table was also where Herb, our son, and his friends brainstormed for physics class and worked on NFL, NBA, American League, and NCAA predictions, pools, trades, and simulated contests.

The cat couldn't resist his curiosity and had risked his life and limb to jump up onto the table once in a while, a no-no.

The table was where I'd served many a homemade pizza or lasagna or pork roast, especially on weekends when Herb's talented-and-gifted class, girls and guys, gathered for a few beers, basketball in the driveway or badminton in the backyard, and a repeat performance of the movie they were obsessed with, *The Big Chill*.

To my ex-husband I delivered the complete collection of Glenn Miller, a gift my mother had purchased from *Reader's Digest*, and the likes of Mel Torme', Stan Kenton, and others. I refused to give him June Christy's *Something Cool,* which included his favorite, "Midnight Sun," because that CD is one of my all-time favorites. I also had delivered to him my mom's sofa bed (almost brand new), the queen-sized bed, and the videotape of *Who's On*

First? with Bud Abbott and Lou Costello. The movie was one of my favorites also, so I found it hard to give up. I handled with care his large framed photograph of his grandfather's graduation class of 1891 from University of Iowa's medical school. He'd been a pioneer doctor in the Willamettte Valley and even a mayor of a town there. My husband looked a lot like him.

Of special importance were the framed Norman Rockwell magazine covers, especially of youthful baseball players, a gift to my ex-husband from Little Leaguers and Babe Ruth. This made me think of my grandfather's first edition of Wendell Willkie's *One World,* stolen long ago. At the bottom of the trunk in the entry, which my sister had antiqued, I found twenty silver dollars that my husband had said were stolen, way back in 1967, by a baby-sitter who happened to be of an immigrant family. I definitely returned those dollars to my ex-husband in their original sock. I gave away the trunk.

I kept the book I gave him March 15, 1975 wherein I wrote, *"Thank you for not turning sour in spite of what the world doth work upon you."* It was David Hapgood's *The Screwing of the Average Man."* He did read it and thereafter fussed many times about the "loss of manufacturing" from American soil. But when all is said and done he was definitely a protégé of President George H.W. Bush's "thousand lights," and volunteered his heart out.

I gradually came to accept that that part of my life was over. I could not make the rest of my life merely one of fond memories. I had to make a new life and continue to live with vigor, and it came to be. My new neighborhood, its people, and their fight to merely survive sometimes—or at the least, to make each day meaningful—I can identify with. I'm at home here and use my room for rent to renew my faith in humanity. I don't give up on human beings easily or readily, regardless. After all, so far I haven't given up on myself, God willing.

At age eleven, I, along with my ten-year-old brother and nine-year-old sister, my grandfather, and my mother, an RN widowed in 1945, stood in the rain for hours to visit the Freedom Train and view the United States Constitution and Bill of Rights first-hand.

In the sixth grade, 1948, I read the energetic and optimistic poetry about American industry by Walt Whitman. As a result, when I saw big trucks and railroad cars in movement it reinforced my pride and confidence, like Whitman's, in my country and my government's capacity to solve problems.

But as a sophisticated, well-read adult, for years when I heard a distant train whistle, I immediately envisioned Jews and Poles lining up and being loaded into cattle cars for Auschwitz and its sister concentration camps. More recently, Hmongs, Uyghurs, Cambodians, and now Syrians—the very obstinate independents of the world, the "untouchables" of every society— are wrongfully viewed as recalcitrant. Although civil disobedience histori- cally has helped their cause or speeded up change, reactionary forces never cease the war against these people's newfound freedoms guaranteed by a fragile legal system that can be downright arbitrary and untrustworthy, that insists on interpreting laws to the detriment of human beings.

Since 2008 at least half of my thirty fellow condo owners are paying double our usual homeowners association monthly dues to cover fees for garbage, water, and exterior maintenance because the other half are not pay- ing their dues, as they are all at various stages of foreclosure. Some have lost their jobs and thus their income. But several are seeking abandonment and foreclosure or just refuse to pay the fees even though they are employed because they resent the loss, the decline of their property values; their mort- gage is now greater than what they can sell their property for.

So I yearn for my childhood version of America: honest, hard-working, and confident in its human energy, and not only with the capacity but the willingness to solve problems created by man, not God.

I live in an area where the disabled suffer birth defects, the working poor grin with missing, malnourished teeth and chronic ailments. They and the immigrants work such long hours in roofing, framing, truck driving, garden- ing, food preparation, and garbage detail that they have no time or access to learn the language or participate in the political process. Their destiny to be American lies in their offspring, if the education system has the capacity to embrace these children and address their dire needs. My area's David Douglas High School bobs along with thirty-plus languages to make brave, absolutely necessary attempts to communicate with the idioms in its midst, in the crowd who aim to have a future in clouding or space travel. Today, Supreme Court justices Scalia, Roberts, and Thomas seem to be totally unaware of this part of my world, which in my view is "We are the majority of humanity, aren't we?"

In our midst there are those who seek escape from their version of misery into drugs they're led to believe by the underworld will provide nirvana. The nirvana merely wastes their bodies and souls. They lose it all. Most of all, they lose control of self, the power to say yes and no, the power to choose, decide.

II. Landlord, Avoid the Ropes and Stay Out of the Corner

CHAPTER TWELVE
October 2011—Sophie

As I got on the #20 bus at 3:00 p.m. after a game of pinochle, there she was, up in front, her face handsome with its strong jaw and straight nose. To Sophie's recollection, her mother, from Austria, was in a wheelchair, suffering from multiple sclerosis. Her father, a larger-than-life Italian, was an opera singer and a volunteer in the Portland Symphonic Choir. He owned a popular hamburger joint on lower Belmont, before the "in" draw that street enjoys today.

Looking like a bag lady, (that is, hauling all her precious possessions with her wherever she goes), riding up front on the bench behind the bus driver, she had a huge purse on her lap and two bulging Fred Meyer shopping bags on the seat on each side of her. Both arms were stretched out to keep guard over the bags.

The bus was full, so I stood at an available spot facing Sophie, who always wore fresh, clean, and warm coats she bought at Goodwill or the very popular Value Village on SE Eighty-Second Avenue. Short and wide with hefty legs, she always seemed to find a blue denim skirt short enough and wide enough.

Right away she asked, "Do you have a renter now?" She was always looking for a place, a better deal, and location was very important to her. "I'm looking for a place. Catholic Charities, they're helping me out."

"That's good," I encouraged.

Sophie had been placed with me in 2004 by mental health specialists. For many years she had been employed by St. Vincent de Paul as a scheduler, over the phone, for pick-up of donations. When that operation closed down, Sophie sold the family home she was living in (the rest of the family was deceased). It was a huge Victorian in the popular, somewhat bohemian Belmont area between SE Twentieth and Thirtieth Avenues. After paying back taxes, she lived on the proceeds and looked for work. When she ran out of money, she was evicted from her apartment. Homeless, she ended up in an Oregon Health and Science University mental ward. The state of Oregon would pay rent to me of $275 per month for her.

For a short time, Sophie had worked in Beaverton for a call center and wanted to go there to pick up a paycheck and look for additional employment. To get there, she said she had to avoid "my cousin's husband, a doctor. He stalks me."

So we'd take the long way, by bus, a two-hour trip, instead of the Blue Max light rail train and connecting bus line, "to fool him, avoid him."

This tended to reveal Sophie's psychosis, further evidenced by her daily behavior, which I was exposed to. She usually left at 11:00 a.m., making food stamps stretch to cover bus tickets. She returned on the last bus at night to our area, out of the city. After watching her DVD of *The Sound of Music* at 1:00 a.m., she would holler and yell intermittently throughout the night at "intrusions" or "intruders."

I reported my observations to her caseworker, who put me in touch with authorities at the state level. They interviewed me for more than an hour. At that time I also pointed out mistreatment of her by others. The very young Dalents next door (racists, narrow-minded, and uneducated but enjoying two incomes at that time) threw her shopping cart into the garbage bin. The night Sophie missed the last bus and took a taxi home, they complained to neighbors, "She's on welfare. I can't afford a taxi. How can she?"

To illustrate how awful these neighbors were, I told how they called the police on me for "making too much noise" with my music three weeks after I moved in. They also called the police when a convict was allowed to visit his mother and sister in the condos. That's when Mrs. Dalent told me, "My family hates blacks and ex-cons. We're Cherokee. We all went to Hawaii in the 1950s for the real estate boom there."

I concluded that, in my opinion, Sophie was no danger to herself or anyone else, but if she would take her medication she would be less tormented, less traumatized. The authorities were able to establish her as disabled and provide monthly income for her.

That was in July, and she began to pay the $275 rent to me on her own. I went to work October 7, 2004, in customer service for a contractor for Nextel. It was a grind-and-grunt job that required sixty-five hours per week for the contractor to meet its "online response" terms with Nextel. The overtime was necessary to the operation because the younger employees with families had to stay home when their children got sick and couldn't go to school or day care.

In November Sophie informed me that she didn't have to pay rent to me anymore since "you have a job, so you don't need my money."

I responded good naturedly but firmly, "No one is allowed to live in my home rent-free other than family. You and I are not related in any way, shape, or form, so, Sophie, you're not family. You must pay me rent every month by the tenth or you can't stay here."

On her $800-per-month disability payments, she took a bus trip to Minneapolis. She felt so welcomed she considered moving there, except for the snow. Next was a trip on Amtrak to California. She called me from San Francisco, saying her money had been stolen. "Wire me two hundred and fifty dollars to get home," she told me. I ignored her plight. She returned home within three days, and I never asked her how she did it.

Physically, she was amazing. Even though very deep-chested and slightly hunchbacked, she could walk miles pushing a grocery cart loaded with her baggage. Sophie rented a storage unit for her antiques, especially vintage costumes, like 1950s formal dresses worn for proms, and antique dolls, the more fragile the better. Her favorite program was *Antiques Roadshow* on OPB, Oregon Public Broadcasting. (She came home early on Mondays to watch it.) She insisted on wearing 100 percent cotton, as it's "more healthy" and "breathes." When I ran into her in 2006 at Starbucks on Twenty-Eighth and Burnside, she told me she had spent the night in her storage unit.

Her skin had a weatherworn but healthy patina; her handsome face didn't look worse for the wear. She used lots of baby oil on her face. I can recall disliking the smell of it even when she cooked her stewed whole chicken with lots of olive oil for hours in too small a pot on top of the range. The baby oil's scent surpassed the smell of the olive oil. What a shame!

Without a rent payment from November 2004, by May 2005 I filed for her eviction. The judge apparently did not empathize with her reason for not paying. When the Multnomah County sheriff came to move her out, she objected and insisted that I was a Scientologist. The sheriff asked me if that was true. It definitely was not true. Sophie's brother had killed himself at age thirty-five, "terrorized by his associations with Scientology," though the family was Catholic. Sophie had found his body in the basement. He had used a gun. So naturally, Scientologists were her dire enemy.

To answer Sophie's question, I told her I had a renter who was employed as a fiber-optics installer.

"How is it living next to a man?" she asked. "I wouldn't like that."

Sophie often imagined a man's face in windows, especially in bathrooms. An incident she told of several times was of a boy, whom she thought was a friend of hers, supposedly watching her through a window in a Wilshire Park restroom in northeast Portland. Those windows are usually very small, extra high up from the ground, and quite often made of mottled glass or just blackened with soil. But glass does seem to reflect images. I remember a robin diving into my den window again and again because he saw the reflection of another bird, itself, on it.

"My renter plays cribbage with me," I quickly retorted to address her concerns about 'living with a man.' "like he used to with his mother. His mother and I are the same age."

I tried to alleviate her fear, assuring her that there was nothing out of the ordinary, male or female. After all, I grew up a tomboy, was on an all-men's water polo team, a starter, at Creston Pool from age thirteen to seventeen, in the afternoons after berry picking. Those guys were my best friends. They're all deceased now. At the ten-year high school reunion, one of the guys, Dave Smith, danced with me. I asked him why the guys never dated me. "You were extra-special, Clancy," he said.

My stop came up, so I gingerly maneuvered through the crowd to get off. I had called earlier to find out the time of connection with the #71 at 122nd and Stark. I had to run to catch it.

"What is your phone number?" I heard her call out as I disembarked.

CHAPTER THIRTEEN

Ramond and Meridith

Sophie was my third renter and a godsend after my experience with Ramond and Meridith (Ramond called her Meri) Par for the course, when I was unable to find a job, I had to put my investment (my home) to work. I understood that renting a room in one's home was not required declarable, taxable income. But the cost and routine of advertising then was beyond me. Instead, I asked around the neighborhood.

A former parole officer with the county was opening up a jazz bar on 112th· next door to a glass company whose manager had befriended me after I inquired with him for employment. The bar owner said he leased the space for his wife, who had experience as a bar manager. He said he had known her since she was twelve. "Such a natural beauty," he told me. "I met her while coaching her brothers at one of the middle schools in northeast Portland." He prided himself in giving her everything she ever asked for.

He knew of a couple—"He's at Benson High School," he said—having trouble finding a place "because they are multiracial. He is on the basketball team, and she is an employed nurse."

Meredith, the nurse, first came to check out the place and loved my home. She was petite, lively, and very pretty. Not too much later on, she reminded me of Janet Carter, my awful neighbor for thirty years, in that she definitely was the decision maker, but in front of her mate she would continually state that he was the decision maker of the family and she would play dumb and helpless.

When they came to move in, his Cadillac Seville stalled in the parking lot, which started things off badly. In 2003 I still had my 1997 Honda, so there was no off-street parking available for his jewel. We all three feared that if he couldn't get his auto started again, it would be towed, as was the homeowners association's routine for misplaced automobiles. Fortunately, a friend of Ramond's arrived, adjusted the problem, and got it started again.

After they paid first month's rent for the furnished room, they insisted on moving in their own furniture: a king-size bed and a huge sofa and chair. Fortunately, they couldn't get the sofa and chair up through the stairwell.

Meri also demanded a key to lock their bedroom and bathroom doors that faced the stair landing, so Patrick, my trusted locksmith from Eighty-Second Avenue, facilitated. A Chinese immigrant, Patrick had put two daughters through the college of pharmacy at Oregon State University. At one time he'd even replaced a lock made in China with an American-manufactured one. "US better made," he said. I had to chuckle.

Ramond did love the huge closet along the entire wall that accommodated his extensive Michael Jordan and Nike wardrobe, with matching tennis shoes for every NBA outfit, in a variety of colors.

Patrick had helped me out after the front door was broken down and my place vandalized on January 18, 2003. Prior to repairs, since the door jamb and frame were gone, Patrick put a long screw into the wall to stabilize the lock. Meridith found a way to reach in the hole from the outside with her tiny hands and undo the lock on the front door.

When rent was due thirty days later, Meridith said she'd lost her job. Then Ramond gave an emotional report as to how his mother was "doing time" (for drugs in her auto while transporting children). Meri's mother, supposedly from Seattle, came to visit. They gave me her mother's check for the rent. The mother insisted on sleeping in the smaller room upstairs but had a small, nervous dog that piddled indiscriminately. A policeman was able to ask her to leave because the association's rules, at that time, did not allow dogs.

I went to Benson High School to inquire regarding Mr. and Mrs. Ramond Smith. I talked with the vice principal, who was very welcoming but avoided giving any answers to my questions. I saw a photo of a basketball team that included Ramond. A friendly student in the administration office confirmed that indeed that "man" was currently on the team. Ramond's last name was not Smith. Ramond had told me he admired Rashad and wanted to play NBA as a small forward. I inquired about Meridith with the office of the director of the certified nursing program but she would not return my call. Her secretary said, "We don't give out information on students." At the same time, she would not confirm Meridith as a student.

Next stop was Mr. Andrew, at a Hollywood (a district in Portland) law firm. He told me about the process at court for evicting them. He said Mr. and Mrs. "Smith" were a racket to take over my home. "Move them out now," he urged me. He gave me this advice at no charge.

When the girl's mother moved out, I asked Meridith for proof of age. Four days later she showed me a California driver's license with her photo. It was delivered the night before, by a fellow with a California license plate on his auto. He humped her, I guessed to pay for the license. I could hear it from my kitchen. Obviously, she was underage. More important, Ramond was in his twenties—over-age for a high school basketball team. He was frequently visited by more than one friend, all female, for one-hour stints.

The mother did not go away far enough. Still angry, she goaded the couple, for being removed from the property. After I filed the eviction paperwork and gave them notice, Ramond and Meri banged on the walls and hammered the plumbing while doing heavy loads of wash, which must have been for their friends, not just them. At one point, the hot water handle broke off while they loaded the washer and water gushed forth, the room flooding rapidly. I was panicked that one of them would get scalded. Meri rushed upstairs to turn off the water at the tank. She knew what to do immediately, like it had been premeditated.

The plumber's bill was the last straw. I became afraid of the couple, so I tried to lock them out the day I paid the plumber. They returned about 9:00 p.m. This time Meri couldn't reach in and unlock the door from outside because I put a broomstick across the door and lodged it into the bar handle on the wall beside the staircase. With the mother-in-law, they hollered and yelled to get in. When they couldn't enter, they went to the back of the condo and began to break one of the dining room windows, which Ramond could reach.

Once the window shattered, with the east wind blowing in, I tried to fight Ramond off with my little rocking chair, a match to my dining set, black with rattan wrapped across the back spokes. (I had sung my son to sleep as a baby in that chair until his feet dragged on the floor.) It is fifty years old and still precious and functional. Ramond grabbed the bottom of the little chair and pulled it to one side, drawing my right hand against the jagged broken glass on the frame of the window. I hung onto the rocker for dear life. I didn't want him to have it. First, he pulled on it, then he reversed direction and pushed it back toward me. His action cut the knuckles on my right hand.

Right then the police came and told me to let Ramond and Meri in. The mother-in-law had left the scene but called the police. Honestly, I didn't have a legal leg to stand on. They were officially still renters and occupants. The police asked no questions and left as soon as I unlocked the sliding doors to the back deck and the Smiths came in. None of us uttered another word. They hurried to their room.

The next day I went to the OHSU clinic on SE Thirty-Ninth and Division and met the director, Dr. Nikolaus. He dressed the wound and reported the attack to the police. He was wonderful. Born in China to Western missionaries, his family shortly thereafter moved to Canada. He found me short in my production of thyroid, so I took on his dose of thyroid medication, which made a big difference. Up to then my hair was thinning. He suggested that, under the circumstances, I was a potential sufferer of PTSD. He recommended a medication, which at the time I turned down.

I don't even take aspirin or keep it on hand. I use salt to sanitize wounds and follow up with a tube of triple antibiotic ointment for rashes and scratches and hurts from my rose bushes and general gardening. I'm deathly afraid of mind-altering drugs, but I do drink beer frequently and wine on occasion. I never seek a condition wherein I would be out of control. Needless to say, I'm careful about the source of a drink per se and "candy," a so-called succulent.

My perfect-sized white Samsonite suitcase—with all those wonderful customs stamps from Hong Kong, Tokyo, Sydney, Manila, Montreal, London, Paris, and Hawaii from my Pan Am days—and my $175-dollar all-wool, three-quarter-length coat from Joseph Magnin, San Francisco, disappeared when the Smiths disappeared. Pumpkin in color, with a huge collar and unique exaggerated half sleeves, that coat looked great with my black, long-sleeve, wool knit sheath dress for special evening events. It was also appropriate for posh weddings or fancy luncheons during the holidays.

The couple in question did not appear in court to defend themselves. The Smiths prepared me for the next two "underworld" characters I would rent to, Rodney and pathetic Wally.

My friend at the glass company on 112th, who specialized in auto glass, put in a temporary dining room window for me. I had proposed the job to him for the money I had, $100. He had to go to a lot of trouble for that amount, I realized. He helped me out big-time.

Probably numbed by the recent events, I actually ended up optimistic. I now had a wonderful new doctor whom I grew to trust implicitly and came to consider a confidant.

CHAPTER FOURTEEN

Rodney

Again unemployed in 2006, I found it necessary to rent out my room. The first response to my ad in *The Oregonian* was an employee with JOIN, a "social service agency." He did not tell me they specialized in ex-cons. He had a client employed with the city's water bureau who was "just getting back on his feet." The agency would pay his rent "until he's able to take it on."

Rodney was a slender African American, five foot ten or so, extremely neat and clean-cut, with even a crease in his starched jeans. He had the cleaners do his laundry.

"Miz Clanzee, you're lak ma swee gran-mon-mon," he said in broken jive to me.

I told him he was on his own for meals, but on Thursdays I would cook dinner for the two of us.

He tried to minimize the importance of his city job, insisting that he was mostly a music producer. He did play his music very loud. He would run two or even three CDs, add a drumbeat with his keyboard console, and try to record them as one product. Through the din I could still hear him incessantly on his cell phone. I had to argue with him to turn down the music. Very significant to me right away: He made lots of sense on the phone—no broken, short jabs of code-like jive talk. He spoke in complete sentences, with purpose, direction, and logical sequence.

On Thursday I made a big pot of spaghetti with wonderful lean ground round from Original Steer a block away. He chatted freely, saying, "Flunked my diabetes test. Won't be able to work." He didn't say it with even an ounce of regret.

I figured he flunked it intentionally and would be fired. Referring to a drug test as a "diabetes test" is a common method among drug addicts to speak of it in front of others outside the culture, like on the bus, rather than calling it what it is—a test for illegal drug intake.

He continued to leave the house at 7:15 a.m. and return at 5:30 p.m. He continued to spend beaucoup time on the phone, and there was no indication of drug use. He was rarely out late at night and was not involved with women or men, but he had lots of incoming calls. He never mentioned another human being or association other than his grandmother. He shared no life experiences whatsoever. He was extremely disciplined, and now I recall that he never ate anything but his cereal with milk in my kitchen. In fact, I never saw him drink anything else other than milk. Very shortly I realized he was not a druggie but a dealer, and well connected. It had taken him less than three days to plug in. He had an auto, a room in a highly desirable location with easy access to a potentially large market, a phone, a source, and a supposed cover as an incurable addict, which I highly doubted; he was in business again.

I called the agent at JOIN but his voice mail said he was on vacation for a week. So I wrote a long letter, with detailed description, to Officer Blink with the Portland police and asked for advice. I got no response, no phone call. To be honest, my major concern was occupying space under the same roof with a drug dealer, a felon. In addition, I am outraged by illicit drug intake.

On the job, a salesperson in late 1979, a leading sales producer—even though he was short, hugely overweight, and often in pain from gallstones—introduced reefer at our crew party in his hotel room. It was let-loose time in Seattle. The reefer got passed around to each of the six salespeople, four men and two females, including me. The other female took a drag as if it were routine for her to do so. Otherwise, she wasn't a smoker. Without indulging, I passed the joint on to the next person in the circle. My lack of action disturbed my fellows greatly. "Come on, now, Clancy," they protested. "What's the deal?"

"Hey, I'm a hooked smoker. I've got an insatiable oral urge. Look at how much I yakkety-yak when I'm not smoking. Plus, my thirteen-year-old is so outraged by drugs that he and the female shortstop on his baseball team threw my three cartons of Marlboros under the house last week. I can't afford another addiction."

My coworkers resented my failure to imbibe, to share their actions. No one talked to me the rest of the weekend at the seminar. Probably they feared that I would report them, and the provider of the marijuana likely feared he would be identified as the source. My job ended within two months, despite my productivity. My fellows no longer considered me a team member to be trusted. Who was I going to tell? But looking back, I should have told the GM who had to fire me.

I told Rodney that I couldn't stand his kind of music, that it interfered with my sporting events and the neighbors were complaining and I was afraid they would call the cops. "They have done so before," I warned.

With no help in sight, it was up to me. One Saturday I was trying to listen to a college football game, the Oregon Ducks, on my TV in the living room. I was sleeping on the nine-foot sofa in the living room rather than in the small bedroom next to his. He blasted his music, and I hollered and yelled. He finally came downstairs.

I told him his unemployment would carry him for a while, even though I knew if he wasn't employed long enough, he wouldn't qualify for unemployment. I offered him $250 out of the $385 in cash to cover a motel until he could find another location. He had made great effort to flatter me, comparing me with his grandmother. Telling him that he made me unhappy, that living in the same household wasn't going to work, cooled his heels.

He took me up on my offer. He was meticulous with his possessions. With care and methodical organization, he put his recording equipment back in its boxes, folded his clothes neatly, and made a place—like a computer-loaded semi in the trucking industry—for everything, very compactly, in his auto. In silence he drove off.

Sometime later the fellow at JOIN actually returned my call. I had left extensive information on his voice mail. He merely said, "I'm amazed Rodney took you up on your offer."

I was going to ask him why he was amazed, but he had to take another call.

CHAPTER FIFTEEN
Lorna, the Butterfly

I ran my ad again. Lorna was a darling girl who wanted to be a child psychologist.

About five foot two and a junior in dress size, she had lived off and on with her boyfriend for six years. She'd met him when she was a sophomore in high school. He had some college and was employed at a mining equipment manufacturer. His posh apartment in the Pearl district was within walking distance of his job. She was working customer service in Beaverton for her father's long-time employer, a recycling division of a very large forest products company. She said the Pearl had a parking problem so she had lots of tickets.

She said she and her boyfriend had to live apart but that she would join him during the week in the early mornings to watch movies with him. She had an overdue account at Netflix. Weekends were "tough," since he spent weekends with his college crowd, insisting that Lorna "go out with the girls."

She claimed she wasn't pregnant. She offered; I didn't ask. "But he's black and beautiful," she told me of her boyfriend. "I would love to have his babies." She actually rolled her eyes back in her head when she said that.

To remain attractive for him, much effort on mod, up-to-date fashions, including undergarments; makeup, including blushes and bronzers; and hair coloring was apparent. She drove great distances, and the cost of operating her auto was "killing." She said the boss had warned her "several times now" that if she were late again, he would have to fire her. She doubted he would do that "because he really likes me," she said.

Her father, Don Murphy, a very kindly, attractive, and concerned fellow, moved her in. He said to me, "Lorna is finally putting it together." Her mother, Stella, from Salem, arrived sometime later to see her place and give her some money. She expressed high hopes for "a new life" for Lorna, as "she has finally left him," she said. I withheld my contradictory information.

To make a short story shorter, Lorna was pregnant, and her longtime boyfriend said it was not his. This was the third time she was pregnant by him. She had lost the first two. At that time she had been working for a large deli in a huge supermarket chain.

She sat at the dining room table, staring out the window, and emoted how "European my skin." She kept saying, "I like me" and "What if, what if?" I stayed my distance. Earlier she had asked me, "I look European, don't I?"

"Yes, definitely," I reinforced.

She decided she didn't want his child after all. She had an abortion and stayed overnight with a girlfriend who accompanied her.

I asked her to leave because she'd lied to me when she moved in. She didn't say how the other two pregnancies had ended. I didn't ask. Now that Lorna was no longer pregnant, her boyfriend allowed her back into his bed. I know this because when I called her cell number at 9:00 p.m., he answered, then turned the call over to Lorna.

An American tragedy, yes, but not a Porgy-and-Bess one where Porgy truly loves Bess. Lorna's mother had made a huge deal about being part Indian and was further frustrated because she couldn't produce a birth certificate necessary for tribal annuities. She had been a social worker but suffered depression and was on disability. Her third husband had suffered from a personality disorder due to an overactive thyroid, but since surgery, he had settled down. He was seeking a disability determination.

Both parents had believed Lorna when she'd told them she was no longer seeing her nemesis of six years now. To complicate things further, Lorna's fellow employee in the office/plant set-up was her father's second and current wife. Reality is more unbelievable than fiction.

When Lorna's boyfriend was in college, he played varsity point guard. At that time he insisted he didn't want her to see him play, so she obediently met him later, long after the game and aftermath of celebration with "his gang." Lorna had never met his family. He avoided hers. She didn't like the fellows, "his gang. They take Del apart from me and drink hard liquor, tons of it," she said.

I call her Butterfly Lady, not only because her fellow made her flit like a moth, but because she taped lovely butterflies she had made all over the walls in her room, at least twelve or thirteen of them, even on the ceiling. They were approximately ten inches long with wingspans of fourteen inches or so, in pastels of chalk or some other soft dust. She possessed loads of perfume bottles, lotions, creams, etcetera, plus the clothes, all over the place. Her décor, I thought, would drive an organized man up a wall.

There are persons in my community who reach out and house the unemployed, the emotionally disturbed, the drug addicts, the down and out. But my mother use to say, "God helps those who help themselves." Lorna treated her job shabbily. She felt it was beneath her. "All I do is Google all day long," she complained. "The job is a cinch."

In behavior and decision-making, she repeated the same scenario, like a playback on the football field again and again. Recently it was found that early sex is dangerous for teens; it stunts their growth. She was a sophomore. She's static.

I have discovered about myself that I avoid relationships where people are inclined to lean on me for help or answers. I have no answers for others. I am so hopeful that they will find answers on their own. Actually, I have great confidence in human beings; I definitely believe that they have the capacity to solve problems created by human beings. But I'm just a sounding board. I don't like to tell other people what to do.

Parents and others, I'm sure, have made great effort on Lorna's behalf. Her father, foreman for eighteen years at his plant, ha stuck his neck out with his employer for a job for her. Who was I to think that now, after everyone's great effort, I could make a difference? I'm not that gutsy or idealistic or egotistical that I could lead myself to believe I could make a difference for Lorna.

She has to get *him* out of her system before she can become a solid, rational being, but one is not going to talk her out of him. She has already paid a huge price to keep him in her life. Her indebtedness included $3,000 for a giant television screen she gave him for Christmas. Lorna wears blinders to win the contest for his bed, to watch one more movie. "He likes the movies I pick," she proudly claimed.

CHAPTER SIXTEEN
Bruce Metcalf

In response to my ad, Bruce Metcalf asked over the phone if he and his fiancée, Sara, could see the room and visit with me on Sunday "to get to know each other."

"Good," I said. "I'll bake a cake. Do you drink coffee or tea?"

"Tea. I'll bring my own. Just boil the H_2O," he said with amusement in his voice.

Of course, I would have them sit in my dining room around the black Formica-top table with a leaf. It is on four legs as opposed to a pedestal; I bought it in 1962. The chairs are especially showy, all-black wood with tall backs, six spokes each, the four middle spokes wrapped in natural rattan. The wood seats are broad and roomy, made more comfortable by yellow-and-white checked cushions on four of the six chairs. A seven-foot bamboo framed étagère with glass shelves sits between the living room and the dining room. A WWII-era credenza of hardwood alder stained dark blond with drawers and shelves—built in Portland, Oregon, and which belonged to my mother-in-law—sits against the opposite wall. Its original top is covered with 12" x 12" inch orange blended marble squares I found at Paulson's. Stainless steel serving pieces—a gravy boat, soup tureen, and fondue set, all gifts from my mother—grace the marble, plus photos of my sister, brother, and son.

To the back sits a large molded-glass vase I won for first place in the novice category at the Portland Rose show last year for the deep pink, forty-five-petal floribunda Ludwig schafen am Rein. That rose bush was suppose to be Robusto, a shrub; luckily, I ended up with a champion, as my research indicates that nothing else has forty-five petals and is deep pink, listed in the 2012 American Rose Society Handbook Selecting Roses..

Above the buffet is a 5' x 5' foot abstract oil by the former department head of the art department at Oregon State College, Munro, which I purchased from the Portland Art Museum in the '60s. My friends used to try to figure out what the artist intended. It looks to me like an elephant and the head of a baby, representing the Republican Party's insistence that a baby be born regardless.

I'm not sure if that party really cares what happens after that child arrives in this world, at least they don't give "it" much consideration unless "he's" a rich heir apparent with wealth to manage, supposedly to "create jobs." Their premise is that the only way jobs can be created is by a rich and clever and, of course, self-made man. Therefore, the entrepreneur's corporations have to be, above all, protected and listened to. Republican spokespeople insist, "Corporations are people, not just a piece of paper that can be bought and sold." In any event, I wish we could ask the artist. In addition to the thought processes it provokes, the painting's saving graces are its magnificent colors and the positioning of the images, the break of the planes.

To the right of the credenza is a small refrigerator, officially in the dining room next to the kitchen. Above the refrigerator is a print from Picasso's Blue Period, *The Tragedy*, which depicts a man, woman, and boy at the seashore, a family seemingly in mourning. It says something special to me. Accepting economic and other realities, I only had one child, a son. Fortunately, he has continued to be a remarkable human being.

In the kitchen there is a white cookie jar with navy puppy paws. It was originally meant to be for dog biscuits. It always makes me think of my friend Ken and his pinochle game. When he bids clubs he always says, "Puppy paws." When he bids spades he says, "Shovels." The other players always know what he means. On the top of the refrigerator, there are recent photos of my oldest grandson and me taken at his first communion, my granddaughter with her dad, my son, as well as a red glass teacher's apple and a timer with a red top.

On the other side of the dining table is a wall of windows looking east through two trees, a linden and a young maple, over grass, and into a cedar fence. On the other side of the fence are nineteen row houses. They replaced a vacant field of Douglas firs and blooming plum trees in 2007. The café curtains are mostly deep red, which complements the reds in the oil abstract and the curtains of mostly red jersey with the same print on both sides of the fabric on the sliding glass door, which lets light through. I made the curtains. There are red, white, and yellow accents, plus an orange teakettle, with a base of navy, blues, and purple mostly in the living room.

In the corner of the dining room is a print of a Chagall painting, faded by exposure to sunlight. I have the same print, though not faded, in the entrance to my den. When my granddaughter was ten, she was big on color, had studied glassmaking, and was fascinated by the condition of the print in the dining room, all the reds and greens of the original reduced to shades of pale blue and white.

A photograph of my beloved grandfather, who died December 2, 1959, sits on the dining table along with potholders that my grandmother crocheted, the only things I have left of her other than a photo of her Hancock High School girls basketball team in 1908, which she coached as a teacher. A daughter of immigrants in South Side Chicago—her father a Prussian Jew mail carrier and her mother an Irish Catholic maid who worked long enough to actually retire from the Armour estate—my grandmother homesteaded Montana with my grandfather in 1909, brought forth nine children, taught school, then became postmistress of Glacier County.

I warned Bruce ahead of time that the doorbell didn't work, so he'd need to knock real hard. At the front door Bruce shook my hand loosely at my fingertips and introduced himself: "Bruce Metcalf, that's an assumed name. My real name is Atsonavorr..." I didn't get all of it. ""It's too long and complicated for people to remember, so I use an easy British name," he explained.

As they entered the living room, they did ask about the six-foot-square red, white, and black geometric painting behind the sofa in the living room. Delighted, I explained, "The art teacher, Robert Brown, at Estacada High School did that for me, framed it, delivered and hung it for fifty dollars. I had beamed, vaulted ceilings in my living room, dining room, and entry in my old house that warranted huge paintings. He promised he wouldn't ever repeat the same size or colors, but it did put him through graduate school in different colors, sizes, and shapes. We collaborated on the original. I brought a page from *Time* magazine—it was in the seventies—for ideas."

I sat on the kitchen side of the table for easy access to serve the cake and tea. I didn't have a teapot but offered one of my ceramic pitchers I used for flowers, somewhat larger than a teapot but shaped similarly, to steep the tea leaves. I had made a Pillsbury white cake in my Bundt pan Saturday afternoon for ease of cutting, frosted it with an extra-large container of Duncan Hines cream cheese icing, and put it in a stainless steel cake storage container my mother gave to me years ago.

Bruce introduced me rather formally to Sara again—"without the H," he noted—and pointed out right away that she was just seventeen. My response immediately was, "She cannot stay overnight in your room, since she is underage. I cannot be responsible in any way for this relationship."

"Her mother, who just finished her master's in nurse management, approves of our engagement," he told me. "We have been counseled by the pastor at their church. Although her family will now be in St. Henry's parish in Gresham, we're going to be married at the cathedral downtown after she turns eighteen. I am a convert," Bruce stated firmly, somewhat on the defensive.

He sat at the table across from me with his back to the windows. His left hand fondled mindlessly, it seemed, her right hand, which was so very small, so white, so childlike, so malleable. Lacking a definable shape, it seemed to be without a bone structure. She was not pretty but not homely, small all over and with no distinguishable features—even, faded coloring; light brown hair, feathery and thin; tiny eye sockets.

When I asked, they said they'd met in an art class at Clackamas Community College.

"You have a lot of art," Sara said. "I have some drawings from class. Would you like to see them?"

"Of course. What class was it?" I was very interested.

"Poster design. Messaging. Persuasion," Sara said, barely audible.

"Sara made a real effective one to convey a message," added Bruce.

"What message?" I asked, still curious.

"That if you don't listen more closely, awful results," he stated.

"What if a person is deaf?" I asked. "Plus, with a poster you are relying on eyes, not ears. Of course, we must also listen with our eyes. I get it, but today's visual uses audio. A poster can't do that, can it?" I was playing with semantics, not like me, being difficult.

"Well, she did have to make an oral presentation with it, that's true," he agreed.

Bruce went out to the car and brought the roll of 6' x 3' butcher paper and stretched it out for us to see. The art was of very crude stickmen and clouds with statements inside. I put on my reading glasses to decipher it. In short: Stop talking. Look, listen, think. Act, don't react.

God help me. A girlfriend who went to charm school her senior year in high school used to say all the time, "Act, don't react." I came to despise that expression, as she turned out to be a real pretender and a very good liar as well. But what stood out was the style of Sara's handwriting: unattractive. It looked like a third grader's attempt at printing letters, uneven and outsized.

Who's your target audience?" I asked to cover up my disappointment. "You know, income, occupation, age, education?"

"Part of the motivation spurs in the workplace," Bruce jumped in to defend the poster, it seemed.

"Is art your major, Sara?"

"I think it will be business," Sara said. "But we're just taking classes now to explore. I like science and math. But I will work and put Bruce through."

Over the phone Bruce had told me he was thirty-two.

"Science and math," I said. "When I did police volunteer work, I found that the juxtaposition of inanimate objects create energy." I wanted their input.

Now Sara began to assert herself. "That's just energy-equals-MC-squared, Einstein's theory of relativity."

"It is?" I hadn't realized that. "I discovered it in the environment of much electronic action. It also applies like the speed of velocity to human behavior due to stimuli, interaction, events, even factors such as persuasion."

They didn't discuss it further. Instead, they returned to eyeing each other with closed mouths turned up at the corners, almost smug, as if saying, "I know, dear, what you are thinking—look." It was like they were advertising to the world or just to me their first, second, third, and fourth choice to merely ogle each other. I have found that the dominant member in a relationship seems to operate in this fashion, playing "I only have eyes for you" for an audience and denying the look, giving no response, when they want something.

They left hand in hand, but a short time later, he returned. He wanted to move in the following weekend. To give me a cash deposit, he needed to cash a cashier's check. Since he was new to the area, he asked if I could suggest a store to cash it and ride with him to show him the way. I suggested the Fred Meyer on 148th where I shopped. There was a Chase branch outlet there as well.

As we entered the parking area, the driver in front of us stopped to pick up two women waiting on the curb for him. "Move it, you black scum," Bruce uttered.

"Hey, take it easy," I said softly, but I was very troubled. "What's your problem with blacks?"

"They cost me my job. I was a desk clerk in Hollywood. They brought in prostitutes so the police were always on my back. They closed us down. That's why I'm now in Lake Oswego and have to travel so far. I get free rent there, but I've got to be near Sara. I was hurt by the quota system," he explained. "Since my family is Brahmin, I lost out for university. Untouchables get in, blacker than black. My father is an engineer, New Delhi, even worked at one time for General Electric. They will come for the wedding," he explained.

With Pan American I'd never bid for a trip to India; I'd actually avoided it. I admire Mahatma Gandhi and his fight over the salt tax, Mother Teresa and her black hole of Calcutta, and, lastly, all the thousands of customer service installations for J C Penney, and other companies, over the phone and Internet because the Indian staffers speak English—but for a dollar an hour, if that? Some brave experts, such as those at *Foreign Affairs* bi-monthly, have written that since India, North Korea, Pakistan, Israel, and China have nuclear power, why shouldn't Iran?

A few very powerful men on Wall Street who have been charged recently for insider trading just by happenstance are immigrants from India. They like gold and make up the largest percentage of new immigrants in the USA from any country, so, of course, there would be a larger percentage per capita of bad apples. But my critical view goes way back to the 1950s and '60s.

To be honest, I have mistrusted the male species from India for a long time. In my senior year in high school, in Asian History, I studied the culture of India. That was in 1955, and their birthing practices at that time were anti-human, based on animus religions, superstitions, and fear of the unborn. At delivery time they stuffed the birth canal with leaves and weeds. Presently, the tradition of dowries and the extreme number of kitchen deaths has caused me further concern. How about the rape of children? God help me.

After all these years of so-called modern advances, they still do not have universal education. Their thing for the cow and the Ganges still dominate their twenty-first-century ideology. The Chinese do push for education, elec-trification, postal service, communications, and a welfare system that at least tries to reach out to rural and remote areas.

In the '60s my husband and son and I took a trip from Portland to Los Angeles, stopping each night in Patel motels to watch the Olympics. My husband picked them for some reason; "research," he said. I thought at the time he'd chosen them because they were cheap. Patel is a large Hindu fam-ily that has invested in low-cost motels throughout the US. The noise raised by prostitutes operating next door to our room until 4:00 a.m. kept us awake for more than one night, once in Yreka, on the way down, and again on the way back in Sacramento.

We could hear the dickering over price, the haggling over the exact ser-vices to be provided, even down to time allotted and how many beers or shots of liquor allowed to the, er, guest, visitor. My husband didn't complain to the management because he said the three male customers next door and others who came and went would make life difficult for us. They would retaliate. "We're outnumbered," he'd said.

So I had lots of reservations about this guy, this potential renter. Please don't assume beyond it. I dearly love my condo neighbors, immigrants that include a Chinese family from Saigon, three generations from Bosnia, Christians from Egypt, a couple from Ethiopia and Romania who work long and dedicated hours in foster care, and a truck driver for Providence Hospital and his wife who is a housekeeper for a hotel at River Place from Costa Rica.. The husband of the young family from the Ukraine has built a strong construction-related firm from scratch. He's up early. Disciplined, he investigates every possibility to put his labor and ingenuity to work. I have volunteered at Meals on Wheels with old-time Chinese, Vietnamese, and Russians since 2006.

My very wonderful dentist was born in South Korea. He is a family man and has a DDS from University of Texas. He now has two clinics and has upgraded unsightly buildings into first-class facilities, even with skylights. In my travels on Tri-Met, I have exchanged with persons from at least forty-five countries, and I'm still counting. Our high school, the largest in the state, has earned many awards for opening doors for its students, who speak more than thirty languages. Some of the immigrants are on the football, track, and baseball teams. Many continue to achieve head-of-the-class status. I agree with Microsoft's Bill Gates—there is a lot of unidentified talent out there worldwide.

CHAPTER SEVENTEEN
Two Beautiful Cranes

The next day a fellow called on my advertisement. I told him the room was already rented. "The tenant will move in next Saturday," I said.

Jonathan pleaded, "I've got to find a place. Can't cook in a decent motel, and my girl loves my cooking." He was employed at a large construction company.

Jonathan shelled and prepared giant prawns and stir-fried them with vegetables, as well as fruits and fruit juices, in his electric wok. Samantha, his girl, chopped onions, lemon grass, celery, tomatoes, and Chinese cabbage, then opened two large cans of Lady Elberta peaches and cut a fresh pineapple. He added brown sugar, which I had on hand. It was a superb sweet 'n' sour. He did the brown rice in the pan juices, then invited me to join him and Samantha at my table for the feast.

She was a well-endowed Rubens type—large breasts, slender ribcage, and large, round but firm hips. Five foot eleven, she moved smoothly, speaking in clear but quiet short sentences in a sweet voice with a touch of glee. I tried to ask her questions just to hear her warm, compelling voice.

"Where did you get that top?" I asked. It had a square neckline that, for a change, did not reveal cleavage; rather, it framed a long throat and an attractive clavicle bone structure. Even her nails were normal length, attractive with manicured, understated white tips.

"Can we put the mattress on the floor to watch TV?" he asked.

"No problem, but, please, put it back on the bed when you leave on Friday," I said.

"This is a great place," he said. "Are you sure about the guy who is going to rent from you?"

"No, to be honest," I said. "His fiancée is seventeen, and I'm not comfortable with that. Also, he's a motel clerk, deals with sleazy clientele. It gives him a jaundiced attitude. He seems to flaunt his Catholicism, acts like it makes him exceptional, acceptable, anywhere," I revealed.

Jonathan lamented his failed relationship with Samantha's nineteen-year-old son. "I work hard every day, pay all the bills. He's unemployed, not looking for work, plays his music real loud so we can't even hear the television into all hours of the night. He bad-mouths his mother. I become very angry, too angry. It scares me."

He continued, "If I say something, he comes back with 'I was here first. This is my home, not yours.' He hurts my feelings, makes me feel bad."

Jonathan seemed pushed, somewhat panicky. Again, he asked, "Are you sure you want to rent to this fellow?"

"I agreed you can stay until Friday. He moves in Saturday. It's beyond further discussion. Fini."

"OK, OK. I bet he's not black."

Jonathan's comment was not like him. It kind of jolted me. "He's dark. From India. Using a British viceroy's name, or something. Seeking legitimacy? Camouflage? Who knows? Come on, Jonathan, you're not going to claim black versus white to me. First come, and I took his money." I tried to put the situation in cement, beyond further consideration.

"I'm sorry," he said. "I'm just anxious for a good place for Sam and me. This would be perfect."

Pushed, wanting, and almost panicked, like lots of good sex was still not taking him down, he was revved up, like a runner ready for the one-hundred-yard dash. Even with his six-foot-five frame, he moved firmly, as if he was actually slender, though he was built more like a football center, albeit a very tall and muscular one. Yes, black, he surely didn't realize how attractive he was in his slim Levis and Nike Jordans.

I was flattered that he liked my place, but I did not consider reneging on the renter, Bruce Metcalf, who had already made arrangements with me. First come, first serve. I would later regret my fair-play stance.

CHAPTER EIGHTEEN

He Took a Shower

Sara and Bruce were apparently an all-family project. When Bruce parked his vehicle to move in, Sara was not the only person accompanying him. Her father, John McTavish, with her brother, John, also drove in, wanting to know where they could park her father's Toyota. All of them except her dad carried the few boxes from Bruce's compact hatchback up the stairs to his room. I stood out in the parking courtyard and chatted with Mr. McTavish. It turned out the father had a bad back and was disabled.

He said that his wife had just finished her master's and found a management position at a major hospital, so they bought a house in Gresham to be closer to her job. "The kids are going to local schools anyway," he said. He talked of his family's fifth-generation role in the parish of the small Willamette Valley town they'd had to leave.

Johnn, her brother, a college sophomore majoring in physics, joined us. The Russian in London dying of isotope exposure was in the news. John readily talked of it. I said, "Chemical vapors and possibly isotopes can be transmitted to target via radio waves."

A tall, teddy-bear type, John asked as his jaw dropped, "Is that why no fluids when flying, like hair spray or hand cream?"

"They don't say, do they? Supposedly, they're the basis for explosives," I said.

John mentioned it to Bruce as he headed for his auto. Bruce just shrugged and didn't stop to respond.

Early that evening I sat in the living room. The big bedroom was just above, and I could hear the toilet. Bruce flushed it again and again. I didn't count, but it must have been as many as twenty times. Of course, I wondered what in hell he was disposing of. Then he banged on the plumbing, which sounded like metal against metal, in the room where the bathtub/shower combination was. It's kind of tricky. You have to pull the lever out from the bathtub faucet when you turn the water on in order to get it to flow out of the overhead shower head. Otherwise, the water merely pours out of the lower faucet into the tub. Finally, he began to shower.

Shortly, the smoke alarm in the downstairs hallway above the washer/dryer began to shriek.-so shrill, so urgent. Right away I figured it was electrical. I panicked. Immediately I dialed 9-1-1 and explained my fears of fire in the walls or ceiling. Everything happened so fast. I could already hear the fire engine. They're only eight blocks from my place. I ran upstairs and banged on the bathroom door.

"Get out of the shower!" I shouted.

Bruce didn't seem to hear me. The shower kept running. I ran back downstairs. Water poured out of the ceiling's fire alarm. The unit went silent. The firemen combed the entire house. I told them about the water out of the fire alarm. They said, "This has got to be a plumbing problem rather than wiring."

Embarrassed, I apologized over and over. "I was so afraid of fire in the walls," I said. "Thank you for such a quick response. I felt I couldn't handle it myself."

At that time Bruce Metcalf sauntered down the stairs, wrapped in merely a towel, and casually said, "What's happening?"

The firemen looked amused. I feared what they were thinking. They probably thought I was involved with this man. I tried to explain, gulping and stuttering along the way—and I don't stutter. "Th-th-this is," I gulped, "Mr. Metcalf, er, from India. He's my new renter, just moved in today."

Without further comment, the firemen disappeared even faster than they had arrived. They probably figured I was just a little off my rocker.

"Go put some clothes on, you jerk," I fumed at Bruce. "I will now have a plumbing repair bill. Good-bye!" I handed him back his check—not yet cashed, not yet endorsed by me. He didn't argue.

He had insisted on putting in the kitchen his bag of rice and a giant cup with METCALF printed on it when there was loads of space for them in his room. When he packed up, I reminded him several times that he must remember to take them. As he started his auto to leave, I ran out to him with the rice and cup. He never lost his cool, friendly demeanor, as if no rejection had ever occurred, as if nothing had happened out of the ordinary. Leaving his cup and rice would have given him excuse for additional contact. How obnoxious. A real gutsy son of a gun.

Looking back, I'm so fortunate that the plumbing leaked, even though it cost me $450 because the repair was on a weekend. There was damage to the shower head and the seal behind it. The incident had instigated a quick and fortunate decision. I hadn't wanted to be a party to the union whatsoever. Six months later Bruce telephoned to invite me to their wedding. I kept it short and aloof. I considered his call rather ludicrous. I don't go to weddings that would make me miserable, dear Lord. There's no joy in Mudville. I struck out.

Sadly enough, I hadn't anticipated that outcome with that renter. Unfortunately, I had no phone number for Jonathan. I learned the hard way. From that time on, I take and keep phone numbers, just in case, for even the remotest possibilities.

CHAPTER NINETEEN
Possibly, An Undercover Cop

For six months I had a first-rate renter—sent from heaven, I swear—from November to June. He was so decent, so disciplined, and, yes, private too, that I began to firmly suspect he was actually an undercover cop on assignment. My suspicions were based mostly on his different autos and a giant, heavy-duty motorcycle he sometimes drove and parked in my off-street carport. Further, his hours on the job were not only at odd times but long and irregular.

Right off, Kurt Krieger mentioned that he needed a place "short-term." I don't require a lease or any long-term commitment from tenants, just thirty days' notice when they're moving out or if my circumstances change so that I must ask the renter to move out.

He had a home in the area. He and his wife were temporarily separated, "although we'll work it out," he offered. When he did move in, with not a lot of paraphernalia, he placed on top of my armoire in his room what I realized was a precious framed photo of his really beautiful wife (dark hair, blue eyes, ivory skin) and two kids, taken on board a cruise ship. I asked him where and when it was taken. He said it was a Carnival cruise, their last, six months ago. "We've taken several. That's our vacation routine," he said. "Even did one to Germany."

He worked for a paper company in Clark County, Washington, that was moving its operation to a new advanced plant downriver, between Rainier and Astoria in Oregon, on the Columbia. His employer was giving him the option of moving to the new plant or getting unemployment and retraining through the displaced worker program. He hesitated to move to Rainier in Columbia County. He purchased a laptop to communicate with the Washington State Employment Security Department in Clark County. He said he wanted to be a parole officer. On his job he was a team leader. He performed computer-wise formula inputs, but his six-foot-six-inch physique (no bulk, bulges, or sags) came in handy because, he said, much of the job was "lifting, moving, and pouring out of huge heavy receptacles to other containers."

With all of my experience, I was sure that a college degree s required for the civil service position of parole officer, but I was reluctant to ever mention that to Kurt. I did assure him that I had worked in classification, job development, testing, selection, and placement for the state of Oregon before I'd gone to graduate school. Sometime later I'd even installed the general aptitude test battery for vocational counseling follow-up at the high school level, so I felt qualified to look for job openings for Kurt. At the time there were lots of jobs published in t *The Oregonian, Clark County Columbian, Asian Reporter,* and the employment departments that he could consider that required engineering, computer, and production skills but not a degree. I cut the notices out or printed them off with the computer at the library and gave them to him. I don't have Internet on my home computer for privacy and budget considerations. The library now allows two hours on their computers in a twenty-four-hour period, which works great for me.

I was very optimistic for him. It was prior to the downturn in the economy, so there was still confidence in future possibilities at that time. Here was an intelligent human being who even spoke German (he'd studied it in high school) and had been responsibly employed all of his life. He expressed such confidence in his team members, so I was quite sure they relied on him to deliver, regardless of their mutual goals.

Kurt was definitely a family man. He liked the improvements I had made to my condo. He said he wanted to upgrade one of his family's bathrooms and indicated he would be gone on weekends to do so. He had totally remodeled their kitchen, "cupboards and all," and their other bathroom.

Kurt continued to describe his home improvement projects, sheer joy in his sparse voice: "Terraced the deep slope of the backyard, which I fenced, to fit it for a patio on the first level. I put plants in the middle and a deck for ping-pong and badminton at the bottom, so the birdie and balls don't tumble down the hill. They were quite contained; we didn't have to chase far. Even put the foosball table down there in good weather. The stairs, in my opinion, were a masterpiece and the toughest part of all due to the drainage. Used sand and mason mud between bricks, then planted an ivy-type ground cover to hold the dirt in place above the steps."

I could just picture it. "Makes the half-inch-by-six-feet boards of my do-it-yourself deck look real freshman in comparison," I mused. "But I did scrub it on my hands and knees and then waterproofed it a year ago, honest."

On some Fridays he went to his twelve-year-old son's Little League games. After the team did McDonald's or pizza, he brought the boy to the condo to watch television and spend the night. They lay on the floor and ate popcorn. I would greet them at the front door and ask his son who won and if he got any hits. The boy was very shy, very blond like his father, and not sure how to handle my inquisitiveness, which I thought was friendly but also showed off my knowledge of the sport. I now realize that with his father away from home, this was a very uncomfortable time for him.

I probably came on too strong for the kid; why should he have to answer questions about his game to a woman other than his mother, even though I looked old enough to be his grandmother? I'm sure it was a traumatic time for Kurt's boys. The other son, a nineteen-year-old working in a liquor store, I met only once. He liked his job but preferred to work at a golf course, and he intended to go to college.

One evening I was dumping the ingredients for Mexican chili—including two cans of dark red kidney beans—into my Crock-pot, to start the next morning. I eat a lot of beans, including dried beans, and store them in my pantry in jars, whereas for his lunch, Kurt kept mostly Marie Callender frozen dinners in the freezer top of the refrigerator. He also often used a George Foreman high-heat roaster for chicken and steaks for supper, with a fresh salad. "It takes all the fat out of it in short shrift," he'd explained when he'd first placed the appliance on the floor under my shelves of a bamboo ladder in the pantry. Anyway, I asked Kurt if he would like to share the chili with me the next night.

"I grew up poor and ate lots of beans. Won't ever eat them again," he said.

"But they're sub protein. Cheap, sure, but good for you," I argued.

"I was so poor that when my girlfriend got pregnant, I went to Alaska, got work in the fisheries. She was the daughter of a big apple grower. They wouldn't let me see her. I help toward the girl, now in med school."

His mother had abandoned the family when he was very young. His father had struggled to raise him and his two brothers, so he was very close to his father. The boys all helped to support their father, happily retired at a fishing lake in central Oregon, in the high country. Kurt made the three- to four-hour trip several times, over Mount Hood in the Cascades, to visit him in the six months he was with me.

Kurt was accustomed to reporting essential information without any evidence of emotion, using as few words as possible, as if he had trained with the marines, but he said he had not been in the military. At fifty-one, he had been between wars. He certainly wasn't the type to avoid one. He didn't complicate, like I tend to do. Accustomed to fulfilling the responsibilities of job and family, he took special pride in the vacations the family took, especially the cruises.

Many times he went to work at 3:00 a.m. and was gone for several days. Some weekends he had lots of friends he spent time with, including some women. We would talk often while standing in the kitchen at the end of the day. He had discovered Club 81 on Division on the way to Gresham. He said it was a fun place.

"They have live bands Friday and Saturday," I recalled, "good ones to dance to, but I don't go there. I've found that if I dance with someone, they expect me to go home with them. I just love to dance, nothing more," I shared.

"One of my favorite places is Hooters," he stated.

"I've never been there. Ribs, isn't it? A black friend of mine from North Carolina, who used to advertise her educational service with me, said that Hooters was the best. She's a connoisseur of ribs. It's a crazy name."

Kurt towered above my small refrigerator, a grin on his face, swung his large hands up to his chest, spread them wide open across his upper body, and said at the same time, "Hooters stands for big..."

"Big boobs," I said, laughing. "Dumb me. I thought it came from 'hoot and holler,' Oklahoma style to indicate a western theme. You mean the waitresses, really."

"You betcha," he nodded. "Built. It's not ribs. The ribs were Tony Roma's in the same location before Hooters came in."

I came to trust Kurt Krieger so on occasion I would read to him my current letter to the editor of *The Oregonian*. It was my usual diatribe challenge to the status quo, especially against the domineering, destructive objections of the far right to the Democrats. They were hateful and negative, in my opinion, so in turn I got hateful, maybe, or just sarcastic; interpretation depends on one's source of information.

Of my first effort, Kurt said, "Clancy, you invite trouble to your door by expressing how you really feel about political and economic things. I feel safer by remaining silent, nonplussed, about all this stuff. No wonder you've had intrusion in your garden, probably in your livelihood."

"I'm just practicing my country's guarantee of freedom of speech, Kurt," I said, defending my effort.

"Those who do reveal themselves pay a high price to take advantage of so-called freedom," he concluded.

He was so clean-cut, so whole, an upright gentleman who never once discussed politics. About one month later, I read another one of my letters to the editor for his opinion. This time it was critical of Vice President Cheney's ties to Halliburton and his subcontracted mercenary military.

Kurt said, "You're exposing yourself, by using your real name, to lots of hate groups, Clancy! There are people opposed to your basically scientific and practical kind of thinking, including the so-called Christian crowd, as well as big, powerful corporations. I avoid extremists by keeping my opinions to myself. If they don't know what I believe, they have no reason to target their animosity in my direction."

"If you don't share opinions with others, how do you choose friends?" I asked.

"Mutual activities and interests, like travel, baseball, TV shows, music, fishing, my kids," he listed. "Friendships based on mutual hatreds, animosities, or passions for or against, I avoid. Too deep for me."

I held a dichotomy, in conflict, for Kurt. On the one hand, I was sympathetic and had real concern that indeed he was faced with finding a new career and, therefore, the necessity of finding another job. That was further complicated by the fact that all of the parole officers I knew were college graduates, so I assumed that a degree, which he did not have, was a prerequisite.

Still, much of the evidence pointed to his being an undercover cop specializing in drug-operation detection, such as identification of marijuana fields, for one. He did mix and had lots of sources for information. Like the trip to the farm between Corbett and Sandy, out in the boonies, he described to me, supposedly to move a female friend from high school back to her family home. I suspected marijuana was grown there or some such thing, plus he never saw her again. Then there were the trips to Seattle over several days in yet another vehicle (not a new one) I had not seen before, without explanation. Phone calls at 2:00 a.m. in the morning. And his motorcycle appeared only two times, all-black, giant, and sturdy, like a police issue.

Did I wish, for sure, he was a cop? Sure I did; then it would save the fine fellow from the trauma of starting all over at age fifty-one, although I firmly believe that it is a good age to return to school. That's what I should have done, but I had a son in school at that time to rationalize my way out of it. I tend to wish the best fate for others, rather than ill, regardless of how illogical. If my suspicions were true, then I would have no reason to worry for him.

In one of our discussions on behavior, I dredged up the past, saying, "My son used to call me a bleeding-heart liberal and a dingbat, probably a carry-over from my Republican husband's consistent critique of me. I got used to constant criticism, and so probably I'm still on the defensive."

"Sounds logical," he uttered in a subdued voice.

I tend to add two plus two and come up with five. It is possible that I spin vicariously with other people's lives. But for the grace of God, go I.

At the end of a workday in May, Kurt stopped at the midlanding on the staircase with the western sun shining in through the tall windows. I looked up at him from the entry. "My wife is always late," he said flat-out, without further explanation, then headed up the rest of the stairs to his room.

Later that day when he was on a call with his wife, I heard his very desperate plea, his tenor voice—a high voice for such a big fellow—whimpering in an even higher key, "Please, please, don't go on vacation."

Was he hopeful that she would save her vacation for a time when they could spend it together? Or did she have some personal purpose for taking vacation immediately? "Always late" could refer to her menstrual cycle, it occurred to me. She was an officer with a title company. Was it possible that she was pregnant and didn't want to be and he wanted her to carry the baby to term? The crisis in his employment, therefore, would cause him—them—immense stress, more than a normal dose.

But I never inquired, never directly probed for clarification. I tend to do that when I am confronted with anecdotes that remain unexplained for me, especially ones that may seriously affect people's lives. They cause doubts and leave lots of questions unanswered, which causes me to return again and again to ponder. Essentially, it was really none of my business, so I now write what was said and leave it hanging, suspended in the vacuum in which it was dealt to me. That's not fair to my readers, is it? I should be the ultimate investigative reporter for them. But real life is a mystery, isn't it? It leaves more question marks over and above facts or figures.

I've got lots of data for you, some premature analysis, but rarely any facts and figures other than height, weight, and preferences. But I question my perceptions and hesitate to assume anything. Even identities shift gears. Four people viewing and hearing the same thing offer their individual interpretations, each unique to one's own angle and contrary to another's. There are those ready to pounce on one's every utterance in order to twist and turn it. And, yes, to destroy the basic character of the one who had the guts to say it.

There are very few of us who don't make an effort to explain ourselves. Hence, there are lots of books, maybe to explain why I have not failed or, moreover, why I did fail. Those who quit the effort seem to opt for death.

Looking back, Kurt had a point. I find that some tight groups of persons (hate groups and haters for hire) are joined not in their enthusiasm for a positive idea but rather in their mutual hatred and animosity toward other persons. This causes them to gather together, such as those opposed to "foreigners," "minorities," "welfare" (one in seven Americans is now on food stamps), "the handicapped" (mentally and physically), and the "loonies" (the mentally ill). But we all teeter on and off the so-called "reality" wire at some time in our lives. Reality proves that we all have the potential to "go off our rocker" given the right environment to do so, hence the high rate of PTSD among our military with combat experience. But if one's attitudes or conditions can't be identified, slotted, boxed, and categorized, one can run free, unscathed, unfettered, according to Kurt.

In addition to the aggressive hate groups like the Ku Klux Klan, militias, skinheads, and Total Population Control, there are also everyday social cliques out of high school, mind you, who exclude and hold each other dear due to their mutual animosities. The 99 Percent/Occupy movement, in a sense, was responding to the power and machinations of the wealthy in our country who possess 98 percent of production capacity and decision making and anything of value, including the fruits of human labor, which they use exorbitantly to exclude, decide, control, and choose, and which has reduced everyone else's access to opportunity, freedom of choice, and, most of all, a job. The sad part is that you have to be part of a group. I'm more of a loner. Isn't it impossible to organize loners, especially via the social media?

Six months or so later, after he moved out, there was Kurt coming out of Precinct 106, across the street from East Portland Community Center where I play bridge on Tuesdays, noon to 3:00 p.m. He was in a Portland police uniform. Later, I was informed that he was Officer Culbertson.

So I can now put my version of Kurt in cement.

In June Kurt decided to move in with a cousin who was recently injured in an auto accident "because I can help him out." His oldest son helped him move. He also took my cable attachment for the television, probably inadvertently, which I regret. It is the only negative thing I can conjure about the dear fellow.

CHAPTER TWENTY

Riva

On a Saturday in early March at 7:00 p.m., I answered a knock on my front door. It had to be someone who knew that my doorbell didn't work, so I opened the door without hesitation. It was Andy, the president of the condo association.

"There's a strange auto parked in your space," he said.

"That's my new renter's," I immediately explained.

"She has a red Ford, doesn't she? This is a two-door Jaguar, looks vintage, no license plate, at least on the front. Got to be stolen. Come take a look."

I walked the short distance with him to the courtyard and the carports. "Sure 'nuf," I said. "This isn't Riva's. She's gone out with a girlfriend. Someone must have left this just now. Why here?" I wondered aloud.

"To stash it, get it off the street, to come and move it later," Andy suggested.

"This spot I have guaranteed to her. She'll be impossible if it's still here when she returns. We better have it towed. Andy, go ahead and call. I want it out of here before she comes back, otherwise she won't have any place to put hers. I don't want to be responsible for a stolen auto. Thanks for discovering it and letting me know."

I returned to my place. The tow operator arrived shortly and did double-check with me before he hooked up to the Jag.

Riva and I had already gotten off to a bad start. She talked incessantly. Although I'm a good listener and try not to sit in judgment, I still get particular about the subjects discussed. She was a licensed medical aide, fifty-one years old, on call for two agencies. In addition, she "helped" a friend, an owner of a foster care home. Riva told me about that so-called friend's entire family and financial history. That repulsed me. I definitely was not going to confide to such a blabbermouth.

More troubling was her politics. At the most, I was thankful that she did not vote. Recently in Alaska and a Sarah Palin fan, she was an addict of Rush Limbaugh and other "haters for hire" radio performers. She quoted them often: "Drill baby, drill" and "Remove that black alien from our White House." Just as soon as she moved in, she expressed how she was all for Congress passing a "don't pull the plug" bill to keep alive the poor wife in Florida. The husband of the comatose woman wanted to remove the life support from his wife who had lain "out of it" for six years. Her parents opposed it. Then the Republicans in Congress pursued it and threatened to pass laws in support of the parents.

"I am against the right to die," Riva said. "After all, I am paid to administer pain-killers." However alive patients might be, Riva never wanted them to die. She wanted them to live forever so that her job of giving them a shot would persist forever. I asked myself, "How many jobs are dependent on this crap—or should I say criteria?" Later speculation made me realize that Riva may have just suffered from an extreme case of self-preservation. I was shortly to learn that she had hoarder tendencies as well. It turned out she had very little room for others.

There was one more thing that got my curiosity up and, yes, raised my latent ire. She raved about her tax man. "He's Middle Eastern. Did you know they're white?" She gave that information more than once. It turned out I knew him, and I had reason to mistrust him. He was the previous owner of a mail service at the local shopping center. The US Postal Service closed him down, forcing him to sell his business. Riva referred to him as a great friend. "He saves me all kinds of money, like his recent advice on my Victorian Rose business, the expenses and mileage for it, in addition to my job."

When Riva returned at 9:00 p.m., she demanded to know why her friend's Jaguar had been towed. "It belongs to her boyfriend," she said. "It will cost two hundred dollars to retrieve it from the tow company."

Naturally, I felt terrible. Riva had told her friend to leave her auto in her parking space and Riva would drive. This friend, Riva had earlier reported in detail, was a highly visible restaurateur who opened, then sold, successful, exclusive restaurants. The friend further delved into other ventures. That evening they had gone to a beauty salon where Riva served as a model for a cosmetic products demonstration. So my blustering, flailing, pacing renter with the big buttocks and boobs had all that goop on her face. Her facial features were grotesque, in caricature, now exaggerated with false eyelashes; heavily leaded, overwhelmingly arched eyebrows; and eyeliner trying to enlarge the size of fifty-ish, sagging eye sockets. It was all very extreme, very comic. In spite of the tragedy of the situation, I had to swallow the laughter that kept welling up in my belly.

The next morning she hung out the front door and spouted her anger to a neighbor curious about the tow truck he'd witnessed the night before. She called herself "exploited" and "taken advantage of," adding "My space I pay for, I can have anybody use it if I say so," "Renters have no rights," and "The least she could have done is call me and ask." At that time I didn't even have her phone number. She had said she couldn't give it out. "Have to keep it open for on-call," she'd told me. She also had a mailbox already.

This was just the beginning of events and damage that Riva wouldn't report, or maybe not even realize. She didn't ask permission to use or do anything.

For instance, Riva spray-painted a ladder-back chair someone had given her on the patio, in the wind, without newspapers, and on my pink Arizona stone table with wrought iron legs. Then she sanded the table wet when I told her to wait until the weather dried out the stone, which further damaged and discolored it. I'd had to discover both events. She'd never reported either one to me. So was she just sneaky, or maybe a sociopath, unaware of the damage and grievance she caused?

I hesitated to set too many rules for her that naturally she would resent, but early on I did ask, "Please don't put wet glasses and cans on the two cutting boards. They stain."

Her response more than once to that request was puzzling: "I have plenty of cutting boards in storage!"

"It's a small, very organized kitchen," I pleaded.

Her preparations for supper many times turned into a three-hour undertaking. I readjusted my time for my meals because that wide-hipped lady, overwhelming in a small space, was like a hippopotamus butt trying to move fast in my kitchen as if she were a chef out of *Bon Appétit*. Maybe she considered herself an undiscovered Julia Child. I bet she'd never heard of James Beard, who was enormous, with a like appetite.

She intentionally purchased off-brands in cans and jars, claiming them to be extra good. She usually found these items, like mango-flavored canned bananas, in small specialty outlets or in clearance bins. She purchased ionized water from a couple operating out of a house in the neighborhood. The water was contained in plastic bottles left over from her exotic health drinks, such as those containing passion flower, lotus, or rose petal juice; Hidcote St. John's Wort; or Albuquerque cactus juice. Initially, she tried to get all sixteen bottles into the refrigerator. Finally, she agreed with me that they would be safe and accessible enough on the floor of the pantry. She thought everything ought to go in the refrigerator, including unopened canned goods.

She didn't use a cookbook. She became offended when I offered mine for her to use. In addition to *Better Homes and Gardens*, I have eleven notebooks of collections cataloged according to type (cakes, cookies, salads, hors d'oeuvres) and major ingredients (chicken, beef, cranberries, cheese) since 1959 from newspapers, magazines, restaurants, and friends. Many of them have illustrations, which are very helpful, such as for éclairs. "I know how to cook," she huffed and puffed indignantly. I offered my recipe books due to her failures and frustration, especially with cooking squash, parsnips, and eggplant, items that definitely need cooking and timing directions. They would burst in the oven—and guess who cleaned up after them.

She made more work for me. She baked every day, mostly packaged muffins, biscuits, rolls, small cakes to go with dinner, and, to boot, desserts, fruit compotes, again in the oven. She was an expert, it seemed, with the microwave, except she consistently burned popcorn in that one. That odor lingers for a long time. She also found use of my fry pan almost every day. It is stainless steel with a copper bottom. I had to scour it thoroughly since she left the grease scorched in the pan. Contrary to my requests, she insisted on keeping old and wilted sponges on long handles to do dishes to keep her hands from getting wet. She merely ran water, sprayed liquid soap, swiped, and rinsed.

Vegetables, fruits, and even meats were usually in cans, bottles, or how-to-prepare packages. Her attempts with fresh ingredients were disasters waiting to happen. Sadly enough, she didn't always use my pans. One evening the oven was spitting. From upstairs it smelled like meat burning. Riva was in her room, so I checked. The oven was set at 425 degrees. She was cooking a brisket (corned beef) in a tinny, eight-inch-shallow cake pan. The grease was squirting all over hell. I called it to her attention. "Why not use my stainless roast pan?" I asked.

Defiant, she muttered, "You're always criticizing my cooking. I think you're jealous or hungry."

I have some champion rose bushes and enter blooms in the spring and fall Portland rose shows and win ribbons. I bought at Fred Meyer what I thought was Robusto, a shrub rose. It turned out to be LudwigSchafen am Rein, a dark pink bloom with forty-five petals. The forty-five petals gave it away. That's how I found out it was a floribunda. It won a first place trophy in the novice category. My newest rose is Walking on Sunshine, and it has won a first-place award, one step from trophy in the Division II, Floribundas category. Most of my rose bushes are shrubs and floribundas, mostly in pots, no hybrid teas. I am dependent on my generous neighbors for extra space for my gardening. There are seven bushes in the ground and twenty-one in huge pots, qualifying me for the small garden category.

The Oregonian's Thursday gardening section once advised to throw out dead roses, which I did. When I trimmed them, I placed them on the pavement in front of my entry until they were high enough to take to the condo compost. Riva grabbed them up, the wilted roses still alive with their color in the petals, broke off thumbnail-size pieces of the petals, and attempted to reconstruct tiny roses on bent twig wreaths. "Victorian style," she called it.

She did not go through a scientific process of drying. Rather, she glued her concoctions onto the twigs, than sprayed them with thick shellac, all within a period of one to two hours. These were her "works of art." For some time I remained unaware that this spraying process took place on my cement walkway to my front door, "bare-assed." (I mean the cement was bare-assed.) Later I discovered that she used the bathroom counter to do the same thing. She loaded the wreaths with flashy ribbon, bows, and flowers.

When her arts-and-crafts friends commissioned a booth at a show or convention, she would load her fragile "works of art" into her auto to join them.

Further, she joined the local business association, passing herself off as an "artist" in business. The "Victorian" rose wreaths had to sell promptly because in less than two months they shriveled, decayed, and turned black. Such a deal for the buyer. Moreover, she couldn't understand why. Lacquered treatment should preserve them, she thought. She insisted on continuing their display on walls where she had placed them, referring to them as "just dried." Riva expressed how much she thoroughly enjoyed talking to customers about her "art" regardless, even though she rarely sold one wreath. She was disappointed that I didn't buy one and hang it on my wall.

I have art I'm very proud of. This includes beloved prints by Picasso, Kandinsky, and Chagall. When in Tokyo with Pan Am, I found Japanese wood block prints, some by Saito, and a silk-screen copy of a seventeenth-century Chinese painting in gold leaf. I have worked with many dedicated musicians and artists in (eight-to-ten-dollar-per-hour) phone sweatshops and also as a teacher in the public schools, and I've purchased giant abstracts in great colors by art teachers I've worked with. I also have a precious charcoal of Bob Marley by F. Conn, a wonderful black nineteen-year-old I worked with at Sprint/Nextel, and pots by George Hahn, a teacher at the now expanding Oregon College of Art and Craft next to Catlin Gabel School. I also have two Mount Hood Jazz Festival posters, from 1982 and 1983, one featuring a piano on the mountain, the other a piano and trumpet on the lake in front of the mountain. The art I own took the artists hours and hours to create, perhaps a lifetime. My grandchildren's gifts to me of art are also treasured. Their efforts from third grade far surpass Riva's renditions.

I have worked closely with lots of struggling musicians and artists who are extremely talented. Riva was not talented, yet she could pay the exhibit fees to get exposure for her garbage. For some reason I resented that—her gall, her dishonesty, her flawed perception of her "art." A visitor to her exhibit asked her, "Are these roses from your garden?" In reporting this to me, she said with a smug look on her flaccid, chubby face with sagging chin, "I was so clever. I said, 'Just out the front door.'"

CHAPTER TWENTY-ONE
She is Still Here!

In November, fortunately, Riva complained that she was afraid to flush the toilet. It was filling to the brim. She was afraid it would flow over. I brought my handy plunger and headed into the room. To respect a renter's privacy, I do not enter without first asking.

I had trouble making my way through the narrow passageway to the bathroom. I am five foot five, one hundred and thirty pounds, although with flat, oversized feet, but that wasn't the problem. She had stuffed the room full with furniture and so-called objets d'art. Even the wall heater was in jeopardy, which I became aware of right away, with junk too close to it.

I asked, "How are you heating the room?"

She pointed to a narrow, primitive-looking metal box, approximately eight inches tall and three inches wide, saying, "My heater, there by my chair."

"It's plugged into an extension cord," I said. I had wondered how the white cord had disappeared from the kitchen drawer. "Heaters are supposed to be plugged directly into the wall."

"It is a real good one. It was my mother's."

"So it's at least fifty years old," I said, alarmed. "Riva, you need to move your stuff away from the wall heater and use it to warm the room. This room has always been warm and cozy. The electric bill goes sky-high with inefficient portable heaters, and they are a fire hazard, especially that one."

I should have known better. She had related several times about her furniture in a garage at the foster home that had to be moved and how she would have to go to storage to house it and fussed about the cost. But I never, ever saw her carry one item into the room. I usually have a full day away from my home, Monday through Friday.

I insisted she unhook the little portable heater immediately and rearrange things, saying, "There's plenty of storage in the closet and bathroom cupboards still." It seemed that she was one of those who needed everything she owned or wanted in plain sight and accessible, reachable at a moment's notice. Was she just lazy? She also hung clothes on their hangers on the rings and knobs of my precious cherry armoire. A long, drapery-like dress that looked wet hung on the brass curtain rod of the huge window.

Even in this mini-crisis I looked out through the multi-paned window to the linden and young maple trees. Now that they were sans leaves, I could see through them beyond the fence in the backyard, out to tall firs in the distance. Closer in, neighbors' yards were loaded with the encroaching brown of winter. To the right of the windows, I saw that the wall-to-wall closet looked half empty. There was nothing on the upper shelves.

After I succeeded in unplugging the toilet in the bathroom, I went ahead and opened the doors to the huge cabinet under the sink and counter. It was empty. I could hear a buzz, so I looked for the noise. In the next room, where the bathtub was located, the heat lamp was on. I turned it off and chewed her out.

Shortly thereafter, I did check the room. Nothing had changed, so I unplugged the heater and put it at the back of the top shelf of the cupboard in the upstairs hallway, behind the twelve-pack of MD toilet paper. I retrieved my white extension cord and put it back in its drawer. Naturally, she missed it immediately and asked about the heater. I told her I would return "that dangerous antique" when she moved out.

The following weekend she did a huge shopping and loaded both the freezer and refrigerator, leaving both doors ajar. A gallon of guava juice lay on its side on the bottom shelf. There was space for it to sit upright. It kept the door open. Riva had complained about the size of the refrigerator. According to her, for a rental I should have a "huge refrigerator with double doors, like the one at the foster home."

The next morning, a Sunday, I found the open doors because the fridge, only a year old, made a grinding sound. Not only were the doors open, it was pushed against the back wall, so it was stressed. I moved it away from the wall and rearranged her items. She had arranged all of them to the front edge of the shelves for easy reach. There was plenty of room in the back for rearranging. Then I closed the doors tightly. At this point, I wrote a matter-of-fact—unemotional, not angry—note to her calling the situation to her attention, pointing out there was plenty of room in the fridge by "utilizing all of its space and by taking the time to do so." She was kind of a push-and-shove person, that's for sure. She reminded me of Sophie, who was also limited in the spatial relations department.

Riva regularly called my attention to a newsletter that listed the removal of licenses to practice from nurses and related health workers, including medical aides, in the state of Oregon. She seemed to celebrate that bad ones were being discovered and weeded out. Of course, that would mean less competition for her job. She was very righteous and talked of how tempted she was to personally report some whom she suspected. Other than her obvious obsession over her health, she did purchase bottles of wine, which ended up empty in the garbage. The garbage also contained an exorbitant number of unusually large, empty, mostly over-the-counter pill bottles; many of the names on the bottles I didn't recognize. She explained merely that she was being treated for "high blood pressure." When I lived alone, I took a trip once a week to the condo's community garbage bins. Now I took that trip daily.

Since she was on-call with two agencies, she looked for a permanent job. She finally got hired by a large firm that housed and educated autistic children, to dispense the kids' twice daily medications. She was to be in training for ninety days.

All of a sudden, she stopped chattering away. "Under too much pressure," she said as she bounced off the walls or squeezed between the counters in the kitchen to prepare her concoctions. She talked of moving to a nicer neighborhood in Clackamas. She gave a short notice to me, which I was more than willing to go along with.

Two days later she went on a ranting tirade: "Those kids are losers. They'll never amount to anything. What a waste of money." Needless to say, she didn't pass the tests required by her training that she "sweated" every Friday and was let go.

I was highly offended by her interpretation of the condition suffered by the youngsters. I told her about former governor Barbara Roberts's son, who'd gone through that kind of program. "He has been steadily employed as a very trustworthy mail carrier on a very large campus for more than twenty years at Mount Hood Community College."

She shrugged it off, saying, "Big deal."

That was the last straw. My disgust and anger festered.

On the pretext that my cousin needed a place, on March 11 I gave her thirty-five days notice in writing, allowing her to stay to April 15. After reiterating all the advantages of the place, including off-street parking, the garden, and access to services—including the library and recreation center (she swam at East Portland Community Center, or at least she put on a large swimsuit and used the hot tub), plus excellent police, fire, and transit—I explained the arrangement on the half-month's rent, writing, "This is like the arrangement you made with me for half a month in January of last year, when you found other accommodations in a 'better neighborhood' then changed your mind."

Out of necessity, I added, "If you still occupy my home after April 15, I will go to the county courthouse to have the sheriff evict you. You have been reliable in paying your rent, so I will recommend you as a reliable rent-payer."

I continued, writing, "Since you have often related that you have used prior rentals and employers to store your personal belongings, I find it necessary to inform you that if you leave any personal property in my home beyond Sunday, April 17, your belongings will be immediately removed to Goodwill Industries."

I signed my note with "God bless you and good luck."

Riva stopped her yakkity-yak and expressed her anger in more extreme ways. She left range elements on. When she departed for work, she left the door unlocked, both locks. The refrigerator doors, including the freezer, all of a sudden were left ajar again and again.

Through her closed door, I loudly said to her, "You leave the refrigerator door open once more and I'll call the police."

She quickly retorted, "It's not a police matter."

So I told LeeAnn at the police department crime prevention unit, representative for our neighborhood, about Riva. I wanted her advice. She thought that Elders for Action might be able to address the situation. That agency immediately sent legal information regarding rights not only of tenants but of landlords, which included a twenty-four-hour eviction process for "outrageous acts."

Riva demanded my attention too often. She caused me to worry. Her antics kept me awake at night. I had even mentioned my concerns about Riva to my dear doctor. At that time I referred to her as an "institutional mentality," you know, the type that figures "I pay taxes, so I am entitled to throw gum wrappers or Coke cups on the sidewalk." Beyond my usual question of why, which I always belabor myself with, now my questions were "Am I safe? Will the house burn down, all that junk?" I couldn't wait another thirty days for her to be gone.

When she left for an assignment on Wednesday, March 23, I could smell chicken cooking from her room. Of course, I entered. It was in a Crock-pot plugged into an extension cord. I was outraged again. So I unplugged every plug in her room and wrote a twenty-four-hour demand note that she move out for numerous outrageous acts that I reiterated on two pages typed in detail. I posted the note on her door.

She insisted she had to work that weekend so would move out Monday. She had a short moving van with a driver who loaded her stuff, a houseful of furniture lodged in one room. She fussed at him greatly over her belongings. She even wanted him to leave the glass items and other fragile things, which she had lined up on my patio, and come back for them in her auto, "because the road we have to drive on is loaded with potholes." The driver assured her that they would be safe in the truck if she would just wrap them in towels and bedding. Plus, he pointed out, "It's threatening rain." She finally submitted to his suggestions.

More than a year later, in August, I ran into Riva at the library. She enthusiastically told me she was now doing sachets at her artist friends' display booths, as if we were old friends, and asked if I had a renter now, saying her current arrangement was unsatisfactory.

Just five days later, on August 20, she drove up behind me as I was returning home and wanted "just-wilted flowers for my sachets."

I said, "I don't want you in here."

With no reaction on her face, as if I had merely said, "Have a good day" or some other very warm utterance, she merely put her auto in reverse and backed out the two hundred and fifty feet or so to the street. Her anger was rarely verbal, always very physical.

CHAPTER TWENTY-TWO
Wally

With Wally I just got softhearted.

"Walford T. Hale. My friends call me Wally." Over the phone he spoke right up, was sure of himself and up front about his disability. Nine months earlier, he fell one hundred feet, climbing a rock wall at Carver, "without a harness," and broke seven bones, several in his back. "But, I can walk," he stated, "sometimes, use a cane. I am low income but I can afford your rent. Your place is close to my church. I work with the young kids there."

"There are stairs," I explained. "It's on the second floor."

"No problem," he claimed.

His son, Will, moved Wally in on a Saturday because Will worked in sheet metal during the week. Will's wife had abandoned him and a young baby and moved to Las Vegas. Wally, his grandmother, and Wally's ex-wife, Lena, were collaborating to get custody of the grandchild. Lena was a former heroin addict but "wants to get back together now that I have a guaranteed income," Wally freely offered.

He wanted to know where he could put the wheelchair, "in easy to get to storage. I just use it to take the bus and MAX, is all." Since this request was contrary to what he had claimed over the phone, I wasn't too happy about this latest revelation, but beyond shock. I had his son place it in the carport storage unit, a short distance from the front door. "What's new," I thought as a conditioned skepticism set in. With some trepidation, I readied myself for more unheralded events.

That same day he made arrangements with the cable company, in his name, for an enlarged print on his computer because of his poor eye sight, a condition he had before the accident.

In his early forties, with Wally's blond crew cut and fair skin he could pass for a youngster in his twenties. His wide, ready smile, often times, was cut short with a jerk of his jaw, a hunching of the shoulders, wincing with a shot of pain. I had heard that nerve damage will do that. He made great effort to pose, hold his broken, hurting, slight, and angular frame erect and at attention. Making it up the eight stair steps to the first landing confirmed to him that he still had his youthful vigor as he willed to do it without his cane, but with the support of the wooden railing.

I admired his great effort to appear strong and normal. But I was also aware that he relied on painkillers, as he spent much time on his cell phone in an effort to acquire more of them. He was hooked up to an outlet in the area called Urgent Care. That's another reason he wanted to rent in the area, to have ease of access to his provider of painkillers. The #4 bus also took Wally directly there. Also, our #4 bus readily connected with the Green line MAX that went into Clackamas County where his family and friends mostly lived. He especially complained of excruciating pain in the kidney area and frequently claimed that his twenty-four-year old son, Will, "of same blood type" "is going to donate a kidney for me."

Starting out of high school as apprentice in a cabinet shop, unfinished furniture, his happiest days were as a short order cook at Timberline Lodge on Mt. Hood, for skiers in the winter and hikers and tourists in the summer. He also claimed making "big bucks" as a restaurant manager but did not specify any. "I've always lived and worked in the boonies," he said, "dreamed of living in the big city." Always employed, he claimed to be a jack-of-all-trades, always ready to work at anything. He was frustrated being out of a job. Early on, he made me aware of his frustration. He often said, "Alaska always saved the day, but now I can't do what I did there."

"What?" I asked

"Eighteen hours a day in the fisheries."

Initially Wally was hopeful that he could make a living working with kids. Every Sunday he attended his church and took pride in watching over the activity room, set aside for restless youngsters to hide out from the lengthy service, more geared to adults. He also offered to escort youngsters to the movies. Parents, mostly relatives, would pay everyone's way, including the price of popcorn and beverages. A parent would drive, to pick up and deliver. For additional income Wally babysat his son's fourteen-month-old girl. He would call me when he had to stay the night.

Wally graduated from a high school in a small town in the upper Clackamas River where his life revolved around the river, especially in summer. He spent that July on the river. Responsible for nephews and nieces and neighbor children, Wally met up with old high school acquaintances at Carver, a grassy knoll cut out of the rock. "My so-called friends tossed me into the river," he said. "It hurt, in more ways than one. I also got chilled, but I had to watch out for the kids."

Wally described a fellow he connected with on the river from high school, "He's rich."

He gave Wally new hope, a great possibility for his future. This fellow had employees for his "buy and sell" business. According to Wally, his friend "has a two bedroom apartment and several vehicles. The second bedroom is loaded with electronics. He buys from friends and eBay and sells on eBay. He doesn't have a driver's license so he wants to hire me to drive." Wally claimed he had an Alaskan license so wouldn't need to get a learner's permit.

In spite of what was so obvious to me about his friend, Wally quit his babysitting job. He explained that his son's boss hadn't paid Will so his son couldn't pay Wally. At that time Wally said he had some old Hi-tech equipment. "I tried to give it away but no one wanted it," he said, "so I'm offering them to pawn shops on Eighty-second." For the next two to three weeks, Wally faithfully made the journey. In a wheelchair, he must have been very convincing of need, if not of honesty.

Wally liked to cook and invited me for a dinner he would prepare; chili dogs, one of my favorites. He talked about moving to a house, "a place of my own," and got a little bitter when he related, "When I was making big money I helped out my brother and my cousins. They've all got their own home now because of it." At dinner he excitedly told me, "As soon as I get my license, we're taking a pickup to Lake Tahoe. Don't know how long we'll be gone."

"Do you trust this guy, Wally?" I asked.

"The important thing is," he hesitated then stated rather dramatically, "Ivon trusts me."

The next day, as I returned home and gathered my mail at the condo mail box at the street entry I could see Wally in the driver seat of a Chrysler Cruiser across the street. There was another fellow beside him. My first concern was that they had probably been in my house. Secondly, Wally didn't try to get my attention, friendly-like, which Wally tended to do.

All of a sudden Wally shut up and ceased to share. That was all the confirmation I needed to assure me that Wally now realized he had given me information which was reportable. He ceased to complain about his pain. The extreme change in behavior initially caused me to suspect that his "rich" friend had also supplied Wally with marijuana which would cause him further delusions.

At that same time when I went into his room to spray for a batch of ants which, on occasion, seem to hatch out of the woodwork in the corner of his bathroom, the smell of smoke in the bedroom was apparent. "Are you smoking in here? No one smokes in this house!"

In a matter of fact manner, Wally said, "The smoke from the campfires, down on the river, get in my clothes. Won't wash out, even the second time."

Wally did make an effort to tell me when and where he would be taking his driving test, strangely enough. In chattier times he had even told me, "I go blind" "driving at night" from "the lights of the oncoming traffic."

"Sounds like glaucoma," I had said.

"I can't afford to have my eyes checked," he countered.

There was no way, with Wally's eyesight, that he could pass the written test on computer without the enlarged lettering, unless someone else took that test for him. So I wrote a letter to DMV Department of Motor Vehicles on Powell, warning them of the possible imposter due to Wally's sight limits. They called me and told me, "If he passes the tests we have to issue him a license."

I said, "I strongly suspect he's involved with a stolen goods operation."

As soon as I found out he was taking the test in Gresham, I called to notify the Portland outlet of that fact.

Shortly after, Wally said he was moving out. His son came and packed him up and told me he was moving him back to his grandmother's in Estacada. Wally said he got his license but I suspected that didn't happen. It would have been his nature to show it off to me. He left an empty box for an X-Box under the bed and a toilet bowl and bath tub with shower that never got cleaned the three months he was here.

He just wanted a job so bad. He feared that his "kidneys and my legs will both fail" due to the painkillers he took. He reluctantly admitted that his back was extremely stressed from the exertion by his arms to push the manually-operated wheelchair. Fortunately, according to his son, a motorized wheelchair was waiting for him at his grandmother's house, "which is one story."

I write about Wally more than a year after he left, so I have let go of the myriad emotions that he succeeded in dredging up in me at the time. I recall my first impression of him was, he's a fighter, rising above his affliction, as he insisted he was devoted to kids. My area has more than its share of disabled persons, which I am reminded of when I ride the bus or grocery shop or when I volunteer with the old time Chinese, Vietnamese and Russians at Meals on Wheels, a free lunch service for seniors, at East Portland Community Center. So, maybe I should do my part. He had chosen my area, intentionally, it seemed. Further, he was so forthright, talkative, had gumption, and motivated to continue with a meaningful existence. Finally, I was disappointed and downright fearful for him by the choices he was forcing himself, deluding himself, into. In notifying DMV I had a dire sense of urgency. Too, I wanted him out of my home. Finally, briefly saddened, but when it was all over, I was so grateful that he was gone. *What a burden!* "*I'm free again.*"

CHAPTER TWENTY-THREE
Notes Intended For Dr. Nik

May 15, 2011
Dr. Nik:

Did you get my novel(s) and daffodils? I took dafs to my friend at Les Schwab, my dentist, some neighbors, my son's family for Easter, and you, at last.

Jose Montesi rented from me since April 1, a really fine fellow who called the mother of his three children his fiancée. Anna, his fiancée, lives nearby with an aunt and grandmother with his daughters, ages nine, seven, and five. From Merced, California, he had to go back to "controlled" living. He broke his parole on March 23 in Hillsboro. He was cited with speeding and driving with a suspended license. At the time, he was working on a job. He was set up to get his GED and wanted to train as a physician's assistant.

So I have found a renter until October, when I have a guy moving in who'll be turning sixty-two and getting his social security income. He's selling his plasma two times per week and cans and bottles to exist, has Meals on Wheels for lunch. He's clean, straight, has a retail sales background, and is a junior college graduate, but Jose and I had more in common to talk about. The lower middle class is being dropped into the down-and-out level, especially folks fifty and over. I was lucky. It did it to me in 1998. Then there were still some options, some open doors, a lot of production jobs that paid $8–10 dollars per hour.

July 4

I loved Jose. He was definitely an angry twenty-eight-year-old, loused up in a steady job in sheet metal by an industrial injury, the loss of his little finger, which frightened him terribly. The state set him up for retraining. His mother, a beautician, had raised him. She'd left Los Angeles, which he preferred, and moved to the Imperial Valley to be with her people. He was so frustrated, yet, I felt, loaded with potential. At the same time, he had an unrealistic view of his options as he tried to beat the odds, go illegal. Sadly, Jose had no idea who was on his side, but he was in search. He had Anna and some friends over on a Saturday night. They watched a video of Chavez, dictator of Venezuela, in Spanish. They discussed it afterward in English. Shortly after, they left the house. He didn't trust government, including law enforcement, and attached to individual exertion of energy and initiative. That's probably why he liked Ron Paul, whom I personally feel gives an oversimplified message, based on Ayn Rand. I prefer John Donne's *No Man Is an Island.*

Jose ordered sex films from Comcast. One week after he left I got a bill for $48. When I reluctantly paid it, I did write to Comcast my explanation as to who ordered those films. I didn't order them.

My new renter, whose 1994 Silverado Suburban with 126,000 miles on it sports Connecticut plates and whose company is subcontracted with a cable company to install fiber optics, found on Jose's abandoned cell phone photos of Jose mainlining heroin. Jose must have done it after he'd found out about the latest order from the court, I thought. Strange, I found Riva more threatening than Jose. She was ridiculous, a total waste of humanity, so I'm relieved she doesn't vote.

I should reserve judgment, but this Brian D.—who grew up in Maine, Florida, Colorado, and Wisconsin (due to a large family)—is an absolute delight. His expertise on the job is his ability to climb poles, if necessary, to splice and install fiber optics. At forty-six, a couple of years older than my son, he has great long legs and broad shoulders but a beer belly that bulges. It doesn't sag yet. A barbecue fiend, he grills pork, beef, and bratwurst and feasts on lots of roasted corn on the cob. He loves mushrooms and eats them stewed. He's delighted with the trees, and he enjoys the squirrels and birds from my back deck, in the shade, facing east. He has taken photos of my garden at the entrance of my condo, facing west and south, to send to his mother who has a condo in Denver.

So I am experiencing a respite, a time of normalcy. My bridge partner for Thursday, Dana Hohnstein, a corporate travel agent and doting grandmother of two, gave me a wonderful yellow apron for gardening and a great famous-beer-bottle barbecue apron. I gave the yellow one to Trudy, my daughter-in-law, as she grows tomatoes and the barbecue apron to my son, Herb. I will tell Dana what I did with them. Knowing her, she will want to sew two more for me. She is very generous.

She also gave me three starts for zucchini squash earlier this year. The condo board voted against zucchini in the courtyard plot. They still just want my two roses, William Baffin and Flutterbye, the Zagreb coreopsis, and the Stella de Oro lilies I put in. There's also a hosta, maybe wild, I had nothing to do with.

I gave the zucchini to my semiretired minister I play bridge with on Tuesdays. He lives on an acre in Boring with a view of Mount Hood. They are landscaping their property. Last fall I dug up and gave to him, in four plastic lawn bags, my champion dahlias, along with their tomato cages, to make room for more rose bushes. His wife (a surgical nurse and very rich, who hikes and camps out with other men friends of hers, he says) put them in and covered them with straw to mulch. I have to check with him to find out if they have come back up. I sure hope so.

August

Monday, I finally took the initiative to cut ties with my lecherous, dirty-old-man semiretired minister. I have tolerated his uninvited comments for more than a year now when he gives me a short ride home from bridge, thirty blocks, no more. Sometimes he takes a side trip to WinCo if he's cooking that evening. He says things to me such as "your cute little butt" and "Your breasts are marvelous with that seat belt between them." Once he actually reached over and put his hand on the seat belt dividing my left breast from my right.

I dress modestly, usually further covering myself with a light jacket. He takes every opportunity to hug any woman, especially the well-endowed ones. I'm not one of those, I assure you. I prefer to hug on my own terms. I choose the occasion, and I've told him so several times. He doesn't catch on. One time walking down the aisle at WinCo, he tried to put his left hand around my hips. How gauche. So from now and hereafter, I have other plans when he asks if I'm riding with him.

I was reluctant to make that decision because I thought he would change his ways; most men do when one does not encourage them. He didn't. Seriously, he continued to become even more blatant and aggressive, and I do fear a showdown of some kind, which I do not want to invite. So it's good-bye to an unattractive fellow who thinks he's hot stuff.

I began to suspect that he puts his words to action. The reason I suspect it is the two women who used to come to bridge with him at different times: Nancy ("She takes care of my diabetes and loves my house," he said of her) and Margaret ("Been in Bible study with her for nine years; her husband has been dying for several years, so I took her to Pok Pok," he said of her). Pok Pok, on Division, was *The* Oregonian's restaurant of the year in 2010. Of Thai cuisine, it is very expensive. Neither one of the ladies have been to bridge in more than six months. I'm beginning to figure out why.

His comments include attempts to portray himself as loaded with dough, whereas I suspect he is a heavy drinker and gambler. "Have season tickets and money on the Timbers," he says. He talks often of his poker games at his place at the beach. He is very devious in the game of bridge and tries to fool us. He has reported several times at bridge that the deer eat the dahlias.

I have found that some old men are very needy. Others are absolute darlings and perfect gentlemen. In a relationship, I still like to learn and share learning—mostly economics and politics—whether my companion is female or male. Some old women are still looking for someone to love them. That's pie in the sky, as far as I'm concerned, balderdash.

August 15, 2011
Copy of my letter to *The Oregonian*
Dear Editor:

"Corporations are people," according to Mitt Romney, a candidate for president of my beloved country. Can you feel their pulse, take their blood pressure, test their DNA? How ludicrous. A corporation is a piece of paper. It doesn't necessarily have to "hire" any people; it is created and used by individuals, even potential slavers. It is not human; only laws and governments and other persons in positions of decision-making, often selected by the people, can give it "life." A corporation can "hire" or even "buy" other persons to make decisions for its favor. How noxious, Mr. Romney; go back to school. What piece of paper (contract) ("people") has bought you? Or are you so rich you merely buy others? Oh, I forgot, your cronies on the Supreme Court backed you up, gave you the impetus, the go-ahead, so you're just exploiting it, using it for all that money coming in from corporations controlled by a few "conservative" people, even though it's contrary to practical, common law. It has encouraged the growth of front organizations, the first of many dangerous negatives to come.

CHAPTER TWENTY-FOUR
More Notes to Dr. Nik

Friday, April 13, 2012
9:30 a.m.
Dear Dr. Nikolaus:

Y ou're a gorgeous (all-encompassing) human being. If I were thirty years younger, I would lust obsessively. But now the need is to share the hurt and injustice and pain of the world, and this is satisfied, almost in overkill. The beauty delivered to me via garden, persons, and the gods of man—these I thank my God for. He is peculiar to me, my very own, as it is for every man. I play Mahalia Jackson's "In the Upper Room," "Didn't It Rain," and "God Put a Rainbow in the Sky" on many a Sunday morning.

I give thanks often for getting to know you via:

• The broken window, executed by an angry black, an irascible Great Pretender who gouged my right hand and sliced the nub of the end knuckle. He was a twenty-two-year-old trying to recoup his NBA ambitions by faking it as a fast forward on Benson High School's basketball team, insisting he was sixteen.

The poisoned, diseased male that could potentially quarantine me, God forbid, and who forced me to deny, disallow, and disinherit Mr. Buckeye, part Siamese. The veterinarian called him a "Blue Point." because of his blue eyes. Why would someone spend chemicals on my cat?

Here's thanks to your wonderful OHSU clinic staff who even entrusted me with their interns. It's been ten years. Hallelujah!

Most of all, you delivered my most precious of all, my son and my family, to me. It keeps me humble for life, so fragile, all so tentative, day by day… Clancy

P.S. Now I must go outside and transplant two new roses, Moon Dance and Walking on Sunshine, and take a dry run to Canby with an eighty-three-year-old with a German accent. He's never been there before, south of Oregon City on the old 99E, east of the river. The town is home to Swan Island Dahlias and Johnson Controls and loaded with loamy, rich soil sans rock of the abundant, prolific Willamette River Valley. We're partners for the annual bridge tournament.

Friday afternoon

At our usual Tuesday bridge gathering of six tables, Otto wanted to drive me home so he would know how to find me for the trip coming up.

First off, I sympathized with his concern regarding the location of my place in a maze of thirty condos that sit deep, back from the road. The street has a standard public name but interchanges with the names of Grant and Sherman depending on what avenue one is on. For instance, at SE Forty-Fifth, the street one block north of Division is Sherman. At 145th, the street one block north of Division is Grant. At 136th, the street one block north of Division is Caruthers.

Secondly, when I invited my ninety-year-old friend, Jean Stayton, another bridge partner, for lunch on a Saturday at my home, she insisted on not one but three trial runs driving me home from bridge so that she could find it and judge the traffic for the safest route. Thus, I'm not in the habit of second-guessing these elderly people with the extra precautions they insist on behind the wheel.

But this eighty-three-year-old gentleman, it turned out, was on quite a mission. With his continental accent and friendly blue eyes, he drove a top of the line Toyota, equipped with the latest "electronics," he went to great lengths to point out. Right off, he was concerned that I rode the bus. He pointed out that in the "over-eighty category in tennis nationally" he was forty-fifth. In doubles with his partner of the same age, they were "seeded fourteenth." Of his wife, he said, "I give her everything she wants, even prime rib at eleven dollars a pound. She knows I'm active, like to go and do, and that's OK with her. She's happy." Then, fortunately, he discussed strategy for our coming bridge game.

Apparently, this guy was up to something. He was a mover. Sadly enough, I would have to shut the door on him, like I did with the minister who put his hands in the wrong places and referred to my "cute little butt." Regurgitate. To make it short, that minister and this Otto must have both assumed that since I was a former stewardess and, of course, didn't own an automobile, that I was on the take to be taken care of or, rather, just an easy lay, prey for some lecherous old man.

We found the Canby Adult Center on Ivy, where the bridge tournament would be held. He wanted to have lunch. Since I've been to Canby before, he said, "Suggest a place."

I gave an excuse, saying, "I knew Canby from 1987 to 1991, when I worked for the newspaper in Oregon City. That was twenty-five years ago." Nevertheless, I directed him to drive toward what use to be the city center of that era to find a place. Canby Pub and Grill, under new management and in an updated building next door to the *Canby Herald*'s office, looked good.

I stated, "I always go dutch. I go to Cleary's Bar and Grill, where I meet friends for a beer every other Thursday, mostly because the bartender, a very good friend of mine, Mattie, works that afternoon. I have a rule. I never accept from anyone an offer to buy me a drink."

"To avoid obligating or involving yourself. So you won't be beholden," he wisely commented.

After looking at the special for the day, we decided on clam chowder if it came with bread. It did. Then he said, "I have no cash, so I will use my card. It'll be a nuisance for the waitress to split up such a tiny bill. You won't owe me."

He mentioned he spoke three languages due to a Polish Catholic mother and a Lutheran German father. He was born in a German town on the Polish border. "I have a good time," he told me. "Went to Hawaii with a fellow. Met a woman there. We had a wonderful time together. I paid all the bills. You and I could do that."

You see, he just wouldn't quit. So I said, "Pan Am crews, we had Waikiki all to ourselves, our own hotel on the grounds of the Royal Hawaiian, took a tunnel to the beach, had macadamia nut pancakes for breakfast in the morning breeze off the ocean, had my first Mai Tai. I avoid ever returning. Then it was pristine, untouched, no development on Diamondhead, no four-lane highways. We took an open jeep surrey ride to the top of the hills to look down on the windward side; could see the towns tucked in on the coast."

"I'm discreet, but it's OK with my wife," he persisted.

I was still being honest with him, but this was developing into a debate so I decided to treat it like one. I've had a wonderful life personally and continue to be mostly grateful. I lack a need to be loved by just any other, other than whom I enjoy currently. My family and friends are enough for me. Most of my old friends are deceased. So I saw an opportunity to brag a little, to put this man back in his place. I am a person who is resented by at least 49 percent of the people in my space and liked by, hopefully, 51 percent of my associates. My niece, Gigi, my sister's oldest of three, is held by most as an inoffensive, lovable treasure. That is not me.

"My husband had severe arteriosclerosis, which affected him mentally and physically. Diagnosed when he was thirty-five, he never told me, for job and insurance purposes. I had to divorce him after thirty-seven years. I was a virgin when I married. I've only slept with one man, my husband, and I intend to keep it that way. My great grandfather was a Jewish immigrant from Prussia. His wife, an Irish Catholic. I like the Ten Commandments. I don't practice adultery.

"I loved another man once, a math professor, but I kissed him only once. We were friends for many years. He was a serious researcher regarding the ozone. In the early seventies, he warned of its depletion and the ultimate warming of the earth. Political opposition moved in on him and destroyed his reputation. He had to change his name and his occupation. He disappeared for a while. Now he is a specialist of baroque music and a leading proponent of classical music. He also loved opera, had a deep sense for the tragic."

Saturday

Now, I thought that was the end of it. Saturday, he insisted on an 8:30 a.m. start time. As we got into his car, my neighbor Esther was just getting out of her van, so I greeted her.

As we started out, I mentioned that Esther, who is black, is one of my best neighbors. "They have another home, she and her brother," I said. "She is a nurse. Her place here is a way station for disabled persons being targeted by organizations like Total Population Control. That includes multiracial newborns rejected by their parents, who are also being targeted by racial purists, which includes TPC again."

"Blacks are OK if they don't get too noisy, loud," he offered.

Oh, God, help me, I thought, *what an offensive, ignorant comment*. "Geez," I said. "Where you been, man, the 1800s? Ever heard of Jackie Robinson? How about our armed forces general who became secretary of state? They're not loud? The teams I root for win, for one thing because their black athletes deliver one hundred fifty percent. My best friend on any job ever was Martha Jones. She climbed up and out of the New York City laundries. Had a sixth sense about people, could always expose the jerks. We cared about the same things—our job, family, and furniture. She was with me when I bought my cherry armoire. I lost her. She died early. Do you even know anyone who is loud and obnoxious at times, other than me? They've got six tons of garbage on their backs—garbage whitey puts there."

He remained oblivious to my challenge and changed the subject. He told of his career in the US Air Force and then at the port authority in procurement. His daughter had a PhD, but was mostly "farming five hundred acres." Their harvest? "Grass seed."

With some knowledge of the subject, I aggressively upstaged him, declaring, "Grass seed use to be the top money-maker for Oregon farmers. Since the downturn in the economy, about 2008, the market has fallen off. Wheat and alfalfa are big. Soft wheat. My family were winter wheat ranchers. Montana, on the Canadian border, hard wheat, semolina. My grandfather, my mother's father, was an agricultural advisor to President Truman, went to southern Italy for the Marshall Plan to recommend a budget for farm implements. As vice president of the National Farmers Union, he organized the grass seed co-ops in Oregon with Mr. Jones in Salem, and Washington at Centralia, in 1947–48."

I offered to confirm to him my informed self and proud heritage, that were not to be demeaned by a silly romp in the sack with a stranger, a married man, to boot. How bizarre. How ludicrous.

"Do you want me to play some music?" he asked as the auto climbed out of Oregon City. I wasn't in the mood for music. In an effort to change the subject, I said it was a shame he couldn't see the Falls, which makes the upper Willamette not too navigable.

"Depends," I went on. "Right now I'm in the mood for Beethoven or Tchaikovsky. My all-time favorite is Chopin. I used to play him on the piano. Never mastered Rachmaninoff." I was intentionally turning the screw. "My friend, the professor with the ozone I mentioned yesterday, our favorite CD was Rampal's *Suite for Flute and Jazz Piano.* Are you familiar?"

While fiddling with the radio, he actually began to sing "Wanting You," then the lyrics "Release me, let me go, I don't love you anymore," his voice cracking, emotional.

Was this to convey, display, his sincerity? I refused to bite. This was ridiculous. But I just commented, "That's an old song, goes way back, to the forties, maybe. Don't hear it in the fifties promotions, *Time-Life,* I don't think."

I wasn't sympathetic. I was resentful. I refused to open the door to his supposed dilemma. It was not my problem or even my concern. But the demonstration did shut me up for a while.

This poor man. Was he really hurting, fighting to be free, to change his life, his commitment, yet at eighty-three? *Poor man,* I said to myself several times.

I chatted freely about my roses.

At bridge we did OK, along with the greater majority, twenty tables times four at each table. But there was a further incident. At lunch break Helmar, also a German immigrant, and his partner, Katrina, who is also

Helmar's new roommate at a retirement home (it's a nice financial arrangement), sat at our table and led the conversation with reports of their new life together. Katrina was ecstatic with her new find. They were like young newlyweds.

After soup, bread, and brownies with coffee, we returned to the tournament for the second round. Our new opponents were some people from our own bridge group. As the couple joined us, Otto blurted out, "Clancy is going to be my wife."

This outraged me. I'm quick to anger at times, especially when my raison d'etre, my reason to be, my reason for existence, my reason for living, my very reputation, is altered by a comment.

"What a foolish statement," I scolded. "You're a bridge partner, nothing more. I just met you. I don't know you from Adam, damn it."

He looked forsaken. Good. What a silly old man.

He briefly—yes, briefly—apologized on the way home. But in his apology, somewhere he alluded to "well, of course, some just masturbate."

I had cooled off somewhat but gave a long story about my time with McGraw-Hill, after I left teaching, 1974 to 1977. "The film product *Free to be You and Me*, for elementary school children and featuring Marlo Thomas and Harry Belafonte, in demand in urban areas, was accused of promoting miscegenation in rural areas. Librarians in forestry towns in the Cascades and southern Oregon told me they'd lose their job even if they just previewed it."

I brought it up to make a last stab at letting him know what was important to me, which was more important in the realm of things than what was seemingly important to him, which was apparently merely making a conquest.

"Churches especially objected to *Free to Be* on the basis that they preach we are born with original sin and have to be taught, controlled, to be good. They object to the theme, the notion, that it's OK to express your unique self apart from authority. I'm sorry, sir, but my son, from the beginning, had an innate sense of right from wrong. I learned from him. He learned by example. For instance, I never told him to say thank you. He said so when he was, yes, thankful," I concluded. A thought finally came to me: Maybe the guy is hard of hearing!

Once home, I was still angry. What do I do to invite this kind of thing? I put up quite a battle. Yes, I felt under attack. And I was thoroughly disgusted by the whole thing. I concluded that the silent treatment in this case would have only served as an invitation. I was sure of it, enough to justify my diatribe.

I so wanted to put him down, insult him, without him fully realizing it until later. Spin circles around him, joust him. My life of effort to be ethical, honest—my very integrity—he wanted to destroy. My reputation, my soul, felt threatened, rather than my mere bod. I was not flattered—just the contrary. I don't see me the way he thought I am. A typical female, I kept talking and talking. Did he actually grasp anything I said? Now I'm embarrassed by the fight I put forth—was it necessary? To fill space till the end of the trip? I was told I am perspicacious, I sense other people's perception of me. He was dead wrong about me—but what took him down that route? That's what boggles. Triggers? I won't cease and desist.

The Pan Am flight crew was mostly WWII veterans with daughters the same age as the flight attendants. They treated us with respect and high expectations and watched out for us abroad, telling us where to shop, dine, and travel, and even accompanied us at times. Maybe once or twice an odd one would ask to spend the night. When I said no, that was the end of it. No further explanation required. No hard feelings.

The after-flight crew party was not intended to be a warm-up for free sex; it was to celebrate another successful trip. After all, this was before the pill. It was the new jet age. International passenger traffic doubled in 1959. The Boeing 707 was the major vehicle out of SFO, San Francisco International Airport, from January 1960. At the time, I took the maiden flight from there to Fairbanks because their runway had been extended.

I remember how angry the crew was in Sydney when a drunken purser brought two prostitutes to the crew party at our hotel. One, Madge, tried to drum up business. I'd sat on the bed and talked to the other, a blond immigrant from Germany. She was in love with an American Indian who flew in twice a year on business for a mining company. "He has no hair on his body," she said. She never took the dates to her place. She raised show dogs, "thoroughbreds." At age twenty-two, I was not interested in types of dogs, so I don't recall what kind of dogs she raised. Now I wish I knew.

Feeling sorry for myself, I decided to take myself out to dinner, which I usually only do twice a month, for budget reasons, but for diet too. I usually go to Don Pedro, Mexican, for a beef burrito with all the condiments—chopped tomato, onion, roasted onions and peppers, hot sauces, radishes, marinated carrots. This time I went to the East Garden Chinese restaurant, which had taken over the large Maverick facility. They offered lunch for $3.98 until 3:00 p.m. and 20 percent off the dinner menu. Their shrimp in hot garlic sauce with hot 'n' sour soup and pork fried rice was absolutely impossible to avoid. We got back in town about 4:00 p.m. It was too late for lunch, but still I indulged, splurged.

Maybe what I should have done was give him the silent treatment, but that's not my style. After a while I had begun to enjoy the debate, the reasons why, I don't know. I think I even told him that I hadn't wanted anyone other than my husband to touch me. Is that the entire crux of the situation? I'm not a great flesh-on-flesh kind of person. Yuk. I mostly made love with all my clothes on. I'm sort of like that prostitute. I prefer less hair, for one thing. Where are you going to find that?

Oh, I have wondered what it would have been like if the Norwegian, Hans Hoyer, in San Francisco and I would have made love. He would hug me hello, that's all. He actually celebrated my cooking. I made real honest-to-goodness large meatballs with spaghetti sauce I cooked all day, like my sister does for her Italian husband. He did ask once to stay the night. I said no. We saw the Kingston Trio at L'Omelette's on El Camino Real in Palo Alto and great blues singers at piano bars in the city. With a master's in physics, he was excited about his job at a major start-up on the Peninsula. But we were both honorable. He had a girl from Cornell University on the East Coast. I had a fellow from college in Portland, Oregon.

My date for the celebration the night before graduation day at Oregon was Muzzie C. We kissed and kissed on the quad until the wee hours of the morning. I recall that evening often, with much good feeling, with lots of what-ifs. He was stationed at Camp Pendleton and we, with a group, got together in Menlo Park when I was in training with Pan Am in San Francisco. He went on to make a small fortune in wheat trading and retired at fifty-five. "How dull," I justify. We had only two dates, not enough to build a life on.

When I divorced I considered seriously making contact with both of them but refrained from making my urges a reality. At the time I believed both of them were married with families. Compared to some, my love life is not worth writing about. I have never ever dreamed of meeting a new somebody to love, to swoop or scoop me off my feet. In a way an event like that scares the hell out of me. I'm stuck in reality. I don't fantasize. The last dream I had in that category was about a fellow who was dead drunk trying to make love to me. I had to laugh about it; what else could I do? Detached somewhat, I see romance as merely complications I don't need. Fortunately, I'm mostly happy, most of the time. In fact, I'm happiest when I'm not in love. Loving someone was painful for me, a real yo-yo trip. His opinion of me became too important to me. My husband's silent treatment was extremely punishing. He convinced me I am tough to love. At the same time, I'm particular as to who loves me. I have had enough action; I don't need any more. Currently, I do not want.

CHAPTER TWENTY-FIVE
Finally, A Normal Renter, Sort of

When I returned home after Chinese food, Brian, my renter, was in the kitchen opening a large jug of Myers's rum. He had reason to celebrate. His company had recognized him, finally. He had gotten a promotion and a raise. That day he was so happy he put a fuel pump in his boss's company truck at no charge. For the boss he liked, that is.

At a meeting with the cable company his company subcontracts, Brian had solved a tough problem of logistics for an installation, how to string fiber optics between two huge houses on Council Crest. Impressed, the cable company engineer had asked Brian, "What are your credentials?" Brian had simply replied, "Sir, I climbed my first pole in 1983."

Brian was ecstatic. He's definitely an emotional guy. When he's exceedingly excited about something, he talks with lots of speed and changes in volume to emphasize key words. Most of the time his speech is short, brief, business-like, and to the point. But he can let go to celebrate good feelings, good times, and that's great. It is not frightening.

Myers's rum is absolutely delicious. I slowly drank two shots while he talked. I rarely drink wine or hard liquor; I stick to beer. The taste and texture reminded me of Remy Martin cognac, my favorite from the Pan Am days.

Eventually Brian asked how the bridge tournament went.

"Four players from our team—there were fourteen of us out of eighty participating—won first and second place," I said. "First place got thirty dollars each, second, ten dollars. Our ten-dollar entry fee paid for the wonderful soup, bread, and even butter, coffee and dessert, the set-up, and the prizes from the drawing at lunch, mostly plants. People from Charbonneau,

Wilsonville, Woodburn, Gladstone, Tualatin, Tigard, Lake Oswego, and Oregon City were there. But it was spoiled by my partner. He wouldn't take no for an answer and argued with me."

"'No' ought to be enough," Brian concurred.

"I'm reminded of something my father told my mother. He wanted her to be sure to tell his kids 'A stiff prick has no conscience.' That describes Otto, or he's merely extremely hard of hearing."

Brian guffawed; it caught him off guard. "In a way that's not me, I guess," he said. "Some women actually thought I was gay because I didn't go to bed with them on the first or even second date."

It was about 8:00 p.m. and dark outside. Brian was still very happy and talking. "Let's go to Pitiful Princess. They're my friends, and I'm celebrating."

Now, Pitiful Princess is a strip bar that Brian had been to at least three times in the year. It's within walking distance, six or seven blocks from my home. I have only been to one of those, er, joints two times in my life.

In 1973 I was the only female salesperson with Dominant Shelf Space when I first left teaching, before I became a media representative with McGraw-Hill's film division. (Outside salespeople used to be *salesmen* in the DOT, Dictionary of Occupational Titles, and retail salespeople were called *salespersons*. That was changed when Women's Lib came on strong. I still use the terminology *man* as all-inclusive of men and women.)

With Dominant Shelf Space, in the beginning my fellow five salesmen in the district were uncomfortable with me. Their wives were especially outraged. Shortly after I was hired by a manager who retired, a new sales manager from Kansas took over the Oregon/Washington region. He didn't relish a green female, a former teacher, on his staff, and of his age, to boot. "Women belong in the kitchen" was the mind-set. But the regional manager, part of the training arm of the organization, was enthusiastic for me and seemed to take it on the chin for me.

At a regional sales meeting in Seattle, my five equals took me to a top-less bar, just for one drink, to show me what it would take to be "one of the boys." Earlier I had told them I grew up a tomboy, since I had a brother who was an athlete. I'd even swum from ages thirteen to seventeen on an all-men's water polo team, as a starter, no less. I tried to be a good sport but didn't look, keeping my eyes on my companions. Finally, we went on to dinner.

For my birthday in 1986, a coworker at the newspaper took me for lunch to a sort of speakeasy in a back alley. A bouncer of sorts greeted him. He seemed proud to be allowed entry and to take me there. I was kind of speechless and looked at the topless dancers a couple of times. It was very dark, and the flashing strobe lights always unnerve me. "The human body is amazing," I uttered. "Not always beautiful, though. I have my own version of what is beautiful in a human being—the body is just part of it."

He said rather sheepishly, "It's a great place for good food.

I don't even recall what was on the menu. His name was Jim. He had five children, and I think his Catholic wife had cut him off sometime back when. He used to criticize an editor he knew who had eight children and no longer lived with his family in Salem, Oregon, although the editor still supported them. Turned out the editor's sole transportation was a bicycle. He provided an automobile for his wife. In any event, I didn't appreciate the birthday luncheon but just changed the subject to advertising prospects, as usual.

But for some reason, I trusted Brian's judgment regarding people, and, yes, I was curious regarding his comfort with the so-called sleazy underworld. He had said of the girls at Pitiful Princess that he "felt sorry for them." He said, "They like me. I'm good to them."

As we walked down Division, Brian was tipsy, in that he kind of rocked from side to side, chattering happily. He was so happy. He stopped at the credit union's ATM and withdrew $60. A slight-of-build and clean-cut, attractive African American in a tailored dark suit, but nevertheless a bouncer type, met us outside the entrance of the all-black, square building with a huge gravel parking lot. "You're awfully happy, Brian," he said.

Brian grinned. "Eaton, this is my landlord, all of seventy-four, Clancy."

Eaton shook my hand. "I'm happy to meet you. I'm the security manager."

I spoke up on Brian's behalf. "He's been celebrating. Had a great day at work. Lots of reasons to celebrate."

"OK, Brian, you're in. But only cola."

It was not real dark. There were no strobe lights. Everyone's face in the room could be seen. The bar, an ordinary L shape, was commanded by a gorgeous woman with a Miss Universe presence, not obviously displaying her boobs or cleavage. I actually enjoyed looking at a beautiful face without being forced to look below her throat. Fortunately, in 2012, it was getting passé in some circles. Now, some women are becoming subtler about their attributes and dressing accordingly. Chests and cleavage and clavicles have been exaggerated; it's been really a big deal since 2005.

Brian got a Coke. I ordered a Bud Light in the bottle and took a seat at the end of the bar.

Eaton stood nearby. I asked of him his experience and attitude toward "all of this." He told me his wife was general manager for all three outlets, which were owned by a Portland man. As a couple they had worked in Las Vegas. She did the hiring. Brian later told me Eaton's wife was Asian and a beauty.

There was a circle of seats at the base of a raised platform in the shape of a horseshoe with a pole in the center. The girls were all slender, and most had small breasts but with seemingly extra-long legs. To make a long story short, there is a bar just north of my Midland County library called The Peephole. I now know why it has the name it does. The girl (one at a time on stage)moves around – to music - then lays on her back and spreads her legs, usually into the air. Then the guys peer usually at the sight between her legs and then tips her with bills the girl tucks into the waistband of her skirt that doesn't cover her fanny entirely. To be more graphic the girl- er dancer - has no other garb on other than that very brief skirt – definitely no under gar-ments. All that money for a peek? You've got to be kidding.

There was a well-built girl with personality at the bar charming an old geezer about the age of my eighty-three-year-old bridge partner. There was just a halter across the middle of her strong, high breasts to cover the nipples. He finally left. She left about 9:30 p.m., smiling and saying good-bye to everyone at the bar, supposedly to make her date. I read it as faked confi-dence. There was some trepidation on her face, as if she needed some kind of reinforcement from her associates. I could sense it or did I just hope that was the case?

The management protects the girls when not onstage from fraternizing with the patrons. They're kept in a room until they dance. I met one of them. She was tall, young, innocent-looking, not overly made up. She looked like a schoolgirl, fragile, not tough or hard. I told her, "How pretty you are." She hugged me lightly, very feminine, very child-like.

Eaton, the security manager, told me they even had some girls in their forties. Why he gave me that information, I have no idea, although they'd been checked recently for hiring underage girls.

One pro-like girl climbed up and down the pole like an acrobat. *I could never do that*, I thought. It made me think of the times my brother, sister, and I would climb the two-story steel stairs at school and slide down the steel support pole to the cement block at the bottom. Once I came down out of control and landed hard on my tailbone. I never tried a pole again. Gripping poles is not an easy task.

I had a second beer, still in my seat at the end of the bar. It gave me a view of the entire room. The crowd was mostly boys, twenty-one to thirty-five, maybe forty. Quite a few escorted women. Brian was forty-six. The patrons were congenial; quite a few knew each other. As a crowd they were decent, well mannered, gentlemanly. A few engaged themselves seriously in the show. I hurried on home at eleven and went right to sleep. Brian came in about one o'clock.

A very good friend of mine, Mattie, a bartender all her life, has known the owner for many years. According to her, his folks, who owned a gentlemen's club, gave him and his brother, when they were in their early twenties, each their own strip club. The one brother, immensely successful, also owned a Christmas tree farm in Estacada. But he got overwhelmed by addiction to drugs and lost everything. The other brother, tall enough for basketball, owns Pitiful Princess and two others. He changes the names of his places from time to time. They have been called names like Snoopy's and Peanut Farm. For me, Pitiful Princess is very telling, very tragic, and says it all without further explanation.

Sunday morning Brian had been shopping and made another find that he took great pride in. He unloaded two large bunches of what looked like old bananas, spotted but still firm. "These were free. They look awful, but they're good inside. You can make your banana nut bread—lots of it—again." I had made sixteen loaves (twelve banana, two prune, two cranberry) between Thanksgiving and Christmas for some of my condo neighbors.

He vigorously peeled and ate one of the bananas. So I tried it. My favorite bananas are still slightly green, not totally ripe, are extra firm, and have a bite to them. This one was soft, real gushy, and too mild. I didn't trust them, since I did not know their origin. Brian shopped at all the way-out (one door in/same door out) freight-damaged lots, the buyout fronts. For his blue jeans, he shopped Goodwill. He found his really great cookbooks at Volunteers of America and a Pyrex measuring cup and frying screen to contain splatters at garage sales.

"Found these on my way to get those kites on closeout," Brian said. He had a new friend, Cal, a coworker. He'd spent the last Sunday with Cal, Cal's wife, Mita, and their nine children, ages six to eighteen. Brian said of them that they're "not rich but leading a great life, happy, loads of energy." He fell in love with them and definitely admired them greatly. They lived on a dead-end street close to Lents Park.

"Every kid has a pet," according to Brian, and "his wife actually chopped wood and barbecued, it seemed forever, hamburgers and—can you believe—twenty-five or more hot dogs. Morning to night means it takes sixty dollars a day to feed everybody. The neighborhood kids all play in their backyard, including a neighbor boy, eleven, with Down syndrome, kind of fat but doing OK. He's just on the edge," Brian further explained as he made a quick gesture to demonstrate, stretching out his right hand flat and rocking it back and forth.

"Marginal, so to speak," I reinforced. "That's great and encouraging." I was impressed that Brian would observe and comment in detail.

He took a long sack into the living room and placed it on the floor as he sat down in the middle of the navy plaid nine-foot sofa, right on the patched cushion. It was the most popular position on the sofa, it seemed. The fibers of its synthetic fabric had worn thin, so I'd patched it with a five-inch-square iron-on in solid navy blue. The upholstery has zippers and can be removed to wash or mend. A millionaire friend has said about the patch that "it's smart-looking, a fashionable treatment, sustaining even. Was it intentional?"

Ha!

Brian pulled out four long, plastic tubes of roll kites, made in China. To his delight there were two kites in the first one he broke open and extra crossbars. As he unraveled them, he said, "Hey, they're not paper. They're silk. Great."

"Gorgeous colors," I said, "naturally." I tried to pick out my favorite.

Then he expressed disappointment. "There are three the same kind; only five of them are all different. For the kids I was hoping for a different design for each one."

"They're all so gorgeous. Such rich, vivid colors. Love the reds, the purples. Look at that orange."

He still spoke with great excitement, fast and breathless almost. "Flew kites as a kid."

"In Maine," I said.

"Yeah," he shot back.

His mother, after he'd had a beer party in their home in Denver, Colorado, had sent him to live with his father on an island off the coast of Maine with no running water. His father was a lobster fisherman, so at age twelve he hauled water and became adept at lobster and scallop harvesting and marketing.

"The winds were fantastic, especially in March, I remember. Once you get it up so high, the trade winds take over. And you have to hang on big-time," he chuckled. "More than once they had me running to hang onto my kite, the pull was so powerful. I have to laugh now. What a thrill!"

"I never got a kite up. On the beach. Ever. I didn't run fast enough, I guess."

"It takes two," he said. "The best way to get them up—good, long string. That's the next thing to find. Two people working together."

He unfurled each kite and installed the crossbar first on one side. There was a notch in the seam at the corners for the stick, about the size of a wooden skewer for barbecuing, to fit from the center post.

"You can keep the kites on the sofa. That's the best place for them," I said.

Brian left the condo, to hunt for string, I guessed. He didn't say. About five o'clock he came out of his room and said, "We're going to take the kites to the kids. You're going too. You'll love them."

He shoved cassette tapes off his right front seat to make a place for me. I had trouble finding all of the seat belt. He was in a rush. He was so excited he was throwing his arms.

At Cal's there were lots of kids. And lots of action, just like Brian said. The six-year-old told me about her coming birthday and the last time she took a tumble, then handed me her cat, asking, "Would you like to hold him?"

I took him against my chest and said, "He looks part-Siamese. They're tricky. Mine bit my friend's nose. He'd get his nose out of joint, get up on shelves, and push big bowls off, which broke."

Mita joined us, saying, "He is a Japanese Bobtail, softer than a Siamese, less feisty."

I got cat hair all over my purple sweater and open black raincoat, but it was worth it. The cat and I got along. Standing close to the entrance, facing the front window, I looked at a glass cage in the corner and a thirty-inch aquarium down the wall from it. Mita introduced me to her eighteen-year-old daughter, just graduated and working.

Another daughter brought a box of cockroaches, moving slowly, which she demonstrated by picking one up. Then she led me to the cage in the corner where there was a horned lizard, looking like a smaller version of a traditional Chinese dragon. "He eats the cockroaches," she explained.

Brian just stood there, listening. I said, "Brian, go get the kites for them so they can fly before dark."

"Nobody tells me what to do," he retorted in a defensive tone, which surprised me.

I aimed to sound real kindly when I said, "But that's why we're here, right?"

All the kids, Brian, and Cal disappeared almost immediately.

So I told Mita about the cockroaches in Houston that our cat who was a stray used to chase, trap, and kill. "Those cockroaches moved as quickly as spiders," I said.

Mita explained, "These are called Himalayan cockroaches and are very docile."

In the fish tank were goldfish and a full-size turtle. "Does the turtle eat the goldfish?" I asked.

"Yes," someone responded.

I mentioned my gardening, especially roses. Mita said she had a rose bush that bloomed all summer, but she was worried about it because it had some yellowing leaves with loads of holes in them. We went outside to see it.

It was a gorgeous, huge rose bush that she didn't even fertilize. It already had buds on it. It was in a pot, a huge one. I assured her it was very healthy but told her what I do with mine. Next to the rose bush, across the front windows, was a huge blooming native of South Africa, a bush that is very hard to grow. It had been damaged from the weight of the snow, which she wasn't very happy about. I assured her that whatever she did was getting good results "so don't be too hard on yourself."

She asked me if it was all right if she smoked.

"By all means, go ahead. I smoked for forty years, but fortunately I was able to quit in July 1996." She asked me how I quit so I told her. "I took five minute smoke breaks at work and puffed and blew without inhaling the cigarette, which satisfied my oral urge, the physical motion. I inhaled each cigarette I lit only one time. Finally, after about five months of that routine, I had removed my nicotine addiction and threw away the pack. Oh, I puffed on pencils for a while. My mother had died the year before on July Fourth. To this day I think she helped me from up above."

Brian and Cal were over in the park. The fourteen-year-old girl played basketball in the street with a temporary hoop set-up. She made most of her baskets. Mita watched the kites go up while we talked. The breeze was slight and there seemed to be no wind high up to really fly high. It was calmer weather than usual for Portland's March, not as much wind and rain.

The neighborhood grade school had burned down, Mita said, and the kids had to go to northeast Portland to another building. Also Marshall High school had closed. Mita didn't want her oldest daughter to go to such a large school as Franklin High, so she applied for her at an alternative school at Foster and Holgate in an old church building. Her daughter got straight A's, had a part-time job working with youngsters, and wanted to go to college.

I asked her about the SAT. Mita had not heard of the SAT. I told her that her daughter ought to take the SAT because it might help her get scholarships. I went away concerned that the mother of nine children had not been informed by the schools of the SAT routine and possibilities connected to it, especially with a daughter with straight A's. I hoped I'd see Mita again.

It turned dark. It was 8:00 p.m. The kite flying ceased. When we gathered again indoors, a Chihuahua, a very healthy one, peeked over the back of the sofa facing a large-screen television. I commented that he was the first Chihuahua I'd seen that wasn't quivering or shivering.

I didn't want to overstay our welcome. I knew they still had chores related to shutting down for the night. "It's a school night, isn't it?" I said. "So we should be going."

Everyone concurred that such was the case. This time Brian didn't object.

CHAPTER TWENTY-SIX
Unwinding

In early July on a Friday at dinnertime, as we both stood in the kitchen having a beer, Brian said, "There won't be a rent check Sunday on the eighth. My good boss is on vacation. My bad boss, his boss, fired me."

"How awful," I said. "You didn't get nasty with him, did you? I know you don't like him."

"No, nothing like that. I have two friends coming from San Antonio. They need a place. But I know, two's too much. I've got some feelers out. I'll know by Thursday. Otherwise, I'm out of here in a week. Will go to Denver. On the way find streams to fish in high mountain Take lots of pizza."

"You mean the Aspen area? Streams that high?" I asked.

"My mother, she misses me." Again and again a tear appeared in the corner of his right eye next to his nose. He kept wiping it away. "My grandmother told me, 'I don't need to worry about you, Brian.' Philippe, the best underground man they've got, quit. He told the boss he found another job that paid sixteen dollars an hour. The big, fat boss says to him, 'So what! I make thirty thousand a month.'"

"So crass, so gross," I said, outraged. "Vote for Obama. He's concerned about the fat cats in control."

"I don't pay any attention to politics, don't vote," he confided.

Like a man without a country, I thought. *Moves around every two years. Says he's been in every state except Alaska and Hawaii.*

"Up to age twelve, I could have been a fat cat. I was spoiled. Had everything a kid could want," he reminisced.

"Then you end up in Maine. Hauling water for survival. Very necessary," I recalled.

"Well, I had a beer party on the sly. My mother had to replace the kitchen carpet," he reiterated. "I was a spoiled rich kid with street smarts. It was good for me. I needed that. Good thing it happened. We went camping three times, with my mom. I remember. She loves camping."

"I hate camping, as you well know," I chimed in. Anything to keep him outpouring, examining.

"She's got a basement. I can live there. Entertainment area, a bar, the whole works."

"You can file for unemployment," I insisted. "Even fired can be disputed. Just have to wait longer for the money to kick in."

"Hate to do this to you," he lamented, returning to the immediate situation of rent due.

I reassured him of my situation, which I usually keep to myself. "I've got savings to fall back on. But I will have to advertise." Looking ahead, I almost pleaded, based on my knowledge of the situation and his habits, "Do me a favor. Clean your tub and shower, the sink and the toilet, or let me do it."

He had refused to let me in his room. Two months after he moved in, I went into his room and cleaned the filthy toilet and sink loaded with whiskers. I actually had to scrub and did send lots of Drano down both drains. I threw out used coffee grounds that he had piled up on the counter and pulled dirty dishes from the top of the cherry armoire and washed them in the kitchen. He was very angry that I did it and said if I did that again, he would move out. At that time there was some evidence he had smoked in the room, so I reminded him, "No smoking in this house. Do I need to say it?"

"You see me. I smoke outside," he had cajoled.

In response to my plea to clean up the place, he said enthusiastically, as if he had just come up with the idea for the first time, "I'll also clean the carpets. Now would be a great time,"

Oh, sure, I thought to myself, *he has been saying that for five months now.*

It was only 6:00 p.m., but he wanted to go to Pitiful Princess "to say good-bye to my friends."

"Would anyone be there now?" I queried.

"Full crew. Don't know when they're closed, for sure."

We walked, crossing Division behind two black males at a crosswalk. Brian was smoking a cigarette, so one of them asked if we had another cigarette. "No," Brian called out, "I roll my own." Unlike the first trip I took with him, this time Brian was very steady on his feet. He did stop at the credit union again and draw out the usual $60. On the way, which was short, I asked him a question: "What did you do with the four hundred dollars for your birthday?" His mother had sent it to him.

He shrugged it off. "Booze, drugs, sex. But remember I won at gambling."

I was not disturbed, even though I suspected he was merely trying to shock me, get a rise out of the staid, naïve old lady, as the saying goes.

This time there was no bouncer to greet us. We walked right in. I took my prior seat at the end of the bar. There was a different bartender, which disappointed me because I was so impressed with the first one I had met. Since Brian or someone covers my bar bill, I decided to splurge and have a gin and tonic. A cocktail is a rare event for me. The bartender asked if there was a gin I preferred. I saw Beefeater in the mirror at the back of the bar. It took me back to my Pan Am days when we served an abundance of it.

A well-endowed blonde took the stool next to me. Immediately I asked her, "Are you a dancer?"

"Yes," she said, "for twenty-two years now."

"I thought you couldn't fraternize, mix with the customers," I said in a quandary.

"That rule only applies to the girls who are under twenty-one," she explained. "For one, they can't drink, and they should be protected."

"You're absolutely beautiful and healthy-looking," I offered. She was probably five foot seven, a size fourteen at least, well endowed, great Doris-Day-like coloring, and revealing only one flaw that I could see. One of her eyeteeth was very small and slightly discolored compared to all of her other teeth, which were orthodontist perfect. She smiled easily.

"I'm definitely not a Twiggy," she laughed. "I'm forty-eight. You're with Brian. I play cribbage with Brian."

"I'm his landlady," I also laughed, "just turned seventy-five. I'm Clancy. Glad to meet you. You remind me of an old friend of mine, Kaye Tomlinson, who is married to Robert Smith, an outstanding former US congressman out of Burns, Oregon. Can you imagine living in Burns? They would trip to Las Vegas in the cold of winter to break it up." I couldn't resist my next comment: "I assume you're Scandinavian?"

"Norwegian and German, but my name is Belinda, not Gerta or Greta." She didn't elaborate further, whereas most people do.

I wanted to keep the conversation going. "Cribbage with Brian. We played only once. He won. He knows every rule that was ever printed about the game, I swear, the nobs, etcetera."

"I'm pretty good. I think that's why he likes to play cards with me."

"How does that set with him?" I was curious.

"Not well," she laughed. "That's why he wants to play again and again."

"He's probably going to Denver next week. He wanted to see his friends here before he leaves. That's why we're here at this time of day," I explained.

It was obvious she was discerning and bright.

"His mother lives in Denver," Belinda continued. "He talks a lot about her. They used to play a lot of cribbage and froze vegetables, made jam, did macramé. He says she was a school teacher but now works as a products demonstrator at MaxControl."

"According to Brian, she's my age," I said. "She was married three times, is real rich because they all died and left her money. He tells me I should be dishonest and pretend I like a guy."

"I can't do that either," she shared.

It's a strain at a bar to look sideways at the person right next to you. Ordinarily I would watch the individual in the mirror on the bar as we conversed. But in my forward view was the clash of colored glass and lights of the bar. Behind us were the usual performers onstage dancing to the drumbeat of standard strip music, which we appeared unaware of. Instead, Belinda and I immersed ourselves in our examination of Brian dePree, a fellow we were obviously both concerned about but surely not in love with. It turned out he had shared as much with Belinda as he had with me, a mere landlord.

"He feels his mother abandoned him when he was twelve," I continued with concern. "He says she admitted that she sent him away because he was cramping her style at that time. It seems that he keeps hoping for a complete reconciliation with her. So now he opts for Denver."

I speculated further by interpreting his past comments. I could visualize how excited he was when he met a tiny blonde who was a homeowner, no less. At times, he would expound on how charming and gentlemanly he could be. "Yes, ma'am," he would say as he bowed and extended his right arm to demonstrate. "You have every right to have me take care of it and I will." Then he'd say of a woman he'd charmed, "I could tell she was really interested in me. She gave me her phone number."

To Belinda I said, "Still, at the same time, I have reason to believe that he's real disappointed he didn't find someone to shack up with. A couple of times he'd get real elated and demonstrative over only three women he'd met who seemed kind of interested in him, but nothing came of them. He lets himself get so shaggy. Looks great when he has his hair cut, only two times since he's been here, in fifteen months."

Belinda was very much in tune, she said. "One night he said he was celebrating his girlfriend's marriage to a serviceman in San Antonio and her move to Kansas because it alleviated his obligation to a rental lease he had signed and was paying every month."

"Early on he told me she had a chronic health condition which I didn't understand," I said, "so I can't remember what it was, although she was a housekeeping manager for a large hotel. He loved her kids. When he found out about the military transfer being able to release them from the lease, all he said was 'I want her to be happy. She was good on her back.'" Now I was filling between the lines. Brian had shared a lot with both of us.

"They all say that, I think to impress that they're great lovers regardless," Belinda interpreted. "Brian tends to be illusionary. Comes with the territory."

I wasn't curious about whether she had slept with him. I figured she had not, so I didn't ask. She wasn't a pitiful princess, just worked there. I did ask her if she had ever been to jail. She said, "My second husband abused me, and I ended up in jail overnight for protection from him. I called the cops on him. Will never marry again. I was afraid of him. It was two a.m., too late for the hospital, they said. The cops didn't know what to do with me. Have you ever been in jail?"

"Almost. That's a story I don't tell. In March 2004 at eleven p.m., I was parked across from Arby's on Halsey, planning to spend the night because my awful next-door neighbors were siphoning my gas. My condo had been brutalized January 18, 2003. Two cops and another man told me to get out of the car, when they don't have a right to do that. I had just gone to the bathroom in my stainless steel six-quart pot, my jeans were down, so I put both arms out the driver's window.

"The short, twitchy cop, dancing around, must have been on something, hit my rear window on the driver's side with his baton and broke it. That did it. Scared the hell out of me. I started the car, drove to 122nd, turned right, and went one hundred miles per hour toward Multnomah County police station, hoping to find a good cop. A county cop saw me and turned around, so I stopped at Glisan and opened the door to get out. The short policeman driving the chase crashed into my fender to break it, even though I was stopped with the door open. The other cop—six foot seven, a good cop, Officer Blink—knew me and approached me. 'Do you want to go to jail or the hospital?' he asked me. I said, 'Not jail.'"

"That's a great story. I'm impressed that you're here in one piece," Belinda extolled.

I stood up to return home. After only two gin and tonics, I felt a little uneasy on my feet. That was not like me. I don't like to be out of control. The new bartender must have loaded my drinks. Two shots of gin would not ordinarily do me in. At the door, Eaton, the assistant manager, met me and walked with me to the street. "My wife and I are looking to get out of this racket. We're hoping to move to Florence."

I jerked as one foot went off the sidewalk. He kindly put his right hand on my left shoulder to steady me as I brought my right foot back onto the cement.

"On the coast, lots of Californians," I said. "That would be great, Eaton. I hope that happens."

I was wobbly so did not ask him what in heck there would be for them in Florence, so I remain curious, but probably will not see Eaton or the Pitiful Princess again in my lifetime. I would enjoy another great chat with Belinda on a subject we both care about. I sure hope such an astute gal is not apolitical. I would bet she's got some damned good opinions.

Amazing is the quality of people like Belinda and Eaton in the underworld. There by choice or circumstance or lack of job opportunities? I hope the best for all of them as fellow countrymen.

CHAPTER TWENTY-SEVEN

Martha

A week later, July 8, the day before Brian would depart, was a sunny Sunday. It was the day scheduled for the condo association board members (I'm vice president) to open up the storage shed and take inventory of the equipment inside. Four of us were to meet at 10:00 a.m. in the parking lot. Martha, the secretary and general organizer, was immediately angry that Nancy, a board member at large, didn't show up.

Brian was also there for added muscle. I had explained to him that the project included a huge, unwieldy aluminum ladder I had once tried to use to inspect my gutters, to remove droppings from my linden, a very messy tree, by the way. Instead, it put a dent in my gutter because it was so heavy. At that time I had to ask Lars, the then current president, to put it back in the shed for me.

I introduced Brian to Martha. Not too long ago, the two had actually had an unpleasant confrontation due to a misunderstanding over her instructions for the striping project of the parking lot. Martha had told everyone in a memo that they had to remove their vehicles from the parking lot on Friday but could park in the Les Schwab lot across the street. The father of a condo dweller told Brian that Les Schwab said that was not true. Martha blew up and told the man off. Brian was in earshot.

"Martha is a Gestapo lady," Brian had said, explaining the incident to me.

"Martha was a purchasing agent for many years for a Japanese hi-tech firm. She's accustomed to making decisions, being in charge," I tried to explain.

Brian continued to report rather adamantly, "She asked my friend Cal, who was waiting in his car for me with two of his girls outside your place, 'Who are you? What are you doing here?' Rude. She's just plain rude. Gestapo. She didn't say who she was or why she was asking."

So I tried to explain Martha's actions. "Next door, Patricia's racing bike was stolen off her back porch, a three-thousand-dollar bicycle. Martha is concerned someone cases the joint. You've lost things out of your van. She thinks she's doing security checks."

"She's just plain rude. Not a friendly bone in her body."

Now, tossing her beauty-shop-curly white hair she had done every Saturday, Martha took the lead. "I said at the last board meeting we can't do this unless everyone shows up," she practically shouted. "This was Nancy's idea to begin with. Now where is Nancy? Her car's not even here."

"Can't Brian take the place of Nancy?" I asked.

Personally, I am very happy every time Nancy drops the ball. As a long-time board member, Nancy has been more than Gestapo. When I had a wall heater installed in my dining room/kitchen area, it had to go on an outside wall due to wall-to-wall windows. As a result, the electrician had to place the wiring through a very small stainless steel tube, up the exterior siding to the attic. He then built a second line for the box, all according to city code.

Nancy discovered the tube on the outside wall and insisted it was against the condo association code. She insisted it be removed. She had the manager of the management firm send me a demand letter stating if it wasn't removed in thirty days, he would remove it. No alternatives were given. I reported it to a Multnomah County judge. Fortunately, the manager suddenly disap-peared. Per the judge's instructions, I submitted to the board my promise that if there were damage or obstructions, I would be financially responsible. I never heard another word about it.

The most recent incident with Nancy involved an Egyptian family next door to her. According to Nasar, who indeed did speak English, even though Nancy never ever spoke to them, "When my baby girl cried in the early morning for her feeding, Nancy banged on the bedroom wall upstairs and yelled, frightening the child." In short, she made the new immigrant family unwelcome. Since then he'd lost his job as cashier at a large gas station, so ultimately had to default on their mortgage. They have since moved—hopefully to a friendlier environment.

Back to the gathering in the parking lot. At this point Martha waved at the driver of a black Buick coming in, who then parked at Dotty's place. Even more excitedly, Martha exclaimed, "It's Dotty's son! He's here to pick up his two kids Dotty is babysitting so that she can help us with the project. I have to tell him he doesn't have to pick them up now because it's not going to happen without Nancy. Thanks everybody for showing up." Finally relinquishing control, Martha shouted, "Maybe next time!" as she rushed over to Dotty's to intercept the driver of the Buick.

As we walked back to our place, Brian said, "I don't like that woman, Martha. She's a dyke."

"She has a daughter, but I think especially she doesn't like men," I said. "She manipulated for a long time to push the president, who was a man, off the board. It's an all-woman board of directors. Isn't that ridiculous? She castrates, doesn't she?"

Dwelling further, Brian tried to explain his complaint. "She came to the door. Right away she said, 'Who told you that we can't park at Les Schwab? Clancy told Dotty that's what you said.' I told her the neighbor with the pickup over there said he asked someone at Les Schwab, who said no."

He went on. "Martha jumps on me, saying, 'Well, that's not true. I personally arranged it with Les Schwab.' Then out of the blue, she says, 'How long have you been here?' I shot back, 'Fifteen months. How long have you been here?' Without another word, like 'Welcome,' 'Have a good day,' or anything, she said smugly, 'Twelve years.' Then, huffy-like, she turned her back to me and rushed off. She doesn't smile. She jabs and gouges and leaves one upset, in a lurch."

CHAPTER TWENTY-EIGHT
Owning Up

On that same Sunday morning, Brian and I each opened a beer: his, a Busch, mine, a Heineken. I had splurged for a new issue of it at Fred Meyer, in cans, not the usual bottles. We sat on the front porch, which looks south on the garden and west to the courtyard. We chatted mostly about the U-Haul truck parked out front getting ready to unload to a condo two doors down from mine. Earlier, the same truck was loaded up, out of Esther's place, with a beautiful double bed, headboard, and footboard. It appeared to be of cherry and a bronze-type metal, plus a mattress and springs, and maybe some other furniture we didn't notice that they drove away with. Now it had returned. Once the doors were open, it revealed immense pieces of dark, mostly black, oversized, ugly furniture. So naturally we were concerned that this furniture was going to replace the beauty that recently departed.

Now, Esther had lived there as long as I had, twelve years, and was one of my favorite people. Reliable and quiet, she was a nurse, working Sundays through Thursdays. She always dressed beautifully for church on Sunday morning before going to work in the afternoon. The man moving in was a boyfriend, which was not a common behavior of hers. Usually, only a beloved brother and many grandchildren, nieces, and nephews visited her home. Martha had put a kibosh on their gas-scooter fun more than a year ago, so the kids kept neighbors at a distance. They would long remember that their scooter-riding in the courtyard and private road were finally forbidden.

I had been made aware of her boyfriend's presence. A friendly guy, Richard reached out, whereas Esther kept to herself. He was big on gardening and sprucing up her place. He had rolled out and installed grass starts behind the garden wall; hung two plants, one on the gated entry; brought in a huge schefflera tree for her living room; and built a rockery for a planter on the inside of the garden wall. On the corner of the turn of the entry, he placed a huge pot with a flowering red rose bush, very showy, very lovely. Plus he had two tiny, happy dogs he would walk on a leash, retaining them behind an accordion guardrail at the front entry attached between the garden walls. And now he was claiming more territory while Esther happened to be away at work.

"That's supposed to be an armoire?" Brian commented on a huge cupboard, black and awkward.

Actually, I feared that this new relationship was to my dear, black neighbor Esther's disadvantage, so I said, "'Assume' makes an ass out of you and me. Just because she slept with him, he moves in on her." I stated some facts at hand to Brian: "That fancy black pickup he drives to his work, that's hers. Now she drives her classic Impala, a gas eater. It used to just sit, parked all the time, as an investment."

Brian stood up and stretched. He took a position at the edge of the porch, between the garden and me. I said, "That coleus and the yellow and pink begonias behind you are absolutely gorgeous, don't you think?"

He didn't respond. He was a big, burly, hairy man, not pleasant to look at, except his eyes were smiley, bright, peering out of all that shag like a rarely groomed Maltese. With a haircut and a shave, he became attractive overnight. Sadly, he didn't realize that, despite my hints in that direction. I would mindfully reinforce him whenever he did shave.

Brian placed his arms outstretched at the elbow in a gesture of oratory. "I might as well be honest," he began. "I lost my employee identification card so had to take a drug test for reinstatement and marijuana showed up, even though I thought I had it covered. So I didn't contest it. I admitted it. Have not been happy with the company. They're cheap screws. The bad boss has me come in Friday—my forty hours are in on Thursday—at three p.m.—ridiculous—to fire me. They have sent managers in Texas using hard stuff—heroin, cocaine—to rehab several times. Same infraction. Workmen's comp pays for it."

146

This didn't surprise me. I got the impression that the bad boss didn't offer rehab and Brian hoped the good boss, who liked him or whom he liked, would offer rehab. Brian had hoped that the good boss, when he returned from vacation the past Thursday, would call him. He never did.

Brian's voice turned to a whine as he walked back across the porch and returned to his white plastic patio chair, which looked kind of skimpy for his large frame. "I'm doomed by heredity," he said. "Have been having awful stomach pains. A disc pops in and out in my back; I can feel it. Have severe chest pains. Grandfather had a stroke at fifty-one. My father had a heart attack early."

"I thought something was up. You haven't been barbecuing. Figured you had an obsession with pepperoni pizza lately," I observed.

"I've always used marijuana. It's especially good here in Oregon."

So Belinda knew what she was talking about when she'd said, "Illusionary. Comes with the territory." Drug addicts lie and lie—mostly to themselves. Looking back on things, Brian had shared events regarding his job performance that had greatly concerned him. Not once, but twice OSHA had ticketed him for the same offense. As a trainer, he failed to have his trainee up in the cage fasten his seat belt to the cage for safety purposes.

Brian insisted on overloading the washer so that it groaned and squealed. I cleaned up after him, especially in the kitchen. He never emptied the dryer vent, so I did so after him. He usually cooked huge meals, like barbecue of two steaks for one meal, letting his dishes, and the ones he used of mine, pile up in his room. Occasionally, he would soak them in the sink, not in the dishpan, forever, it seemed. Then he'd finally rinse them and put them on the drain rack or forget them for several days before doing so. He never wiped down the sink's walls. I'd told Cal's wife, Mita, on kite day, "He's a slob."

Mita'd retorted, "All men are."

Brian sent an "edibles" basket to his mother for her birthday. It cost him eighty dollars. For his birthday she'd sent four hundred dollars in bills of one hundreds and fifties tucked in the breast and shoulder pockets of three T-shirts she bought at MaxControl, where she worked. He was like a little kid in search of the money. It reminded me of his elation with the kids' kites. She also sent a ton of coupons.

He used a contraption to roll his cigarettes, after he placed the tobacco in there. I latently suspected that he actually mixed the marijuana in with his tobacco. What the hell?

"I'm mad at you, Brian," I said. "You had a good thing going. A steady job; first-class, convenient accommodations that didn't cost an arm and a leg; lots of friends like Pat and Darren next door, your cribbage partner, Belinda, Cal and his family, guys at work. And you blew it—to puff a damned weed. Do you wish for death, or do you just dread death?"

"I think I should be on disability for the eight hundred per month," he said. "I could live real good on that. On my way to Denver, I'm going to fish on high mountain streams, away from people."

"Do you need a state's license, like you got for Oregon?" I recalled how concerned he was about out-of-state fees required for an Oregon fishing license. "In fact, Brian, that fishing trip, just a week ago with your new friend, is the last time I've seen you so happy. You were ecstatic over the whole thing, but you couldn't tell me what river or fishing hole it was or where it was at. Fishing in the wilderness! Don't get lost out there. My brother is very critical of people who go hiking and the National Guard is called out to find them."

Brian now rolled, lit, and inhaled one cigarette after another. *Must be what he does in my room*, I thought. *How awful; no wonder it stinks. No wonder he insists I keep out.*

Addiction makes one a liar, a procrastinator, and irresponsible. *The jig is up, so now he tells the truth*, I thought. I realized that he considered his job physically very demanding. But often he expressed loving it, how good he was at it, especially compared to others. He resented authority, but lots of people do. He especially prided himself on how fast he could complete a job compared to others. With the high risk of error and infractions, that was not to be commended, I guessed. A person pushes like that when he or she is insecure in their situation, and he was. Pressure from higher up will do that.

He would complain about thieves in the area, and he lost things out of his van, but he never locked it. Brian lost tools and finally his lunch bucket with his employee identification while parked at Walgreen's. To get rein-stated, he was required to take the entry drug test. He even left his very expensive bicycle out one night. Fortunately, Pat, next door, wheeled it to the backyard and locked it up for him.

"Eventually, I'm going to my mother's, but not right away because they're going to Hawaii in July, she and her current boyfriend," he mused. "I'll fish till then."

What a twist, a turnabout, I thought. "Not long ago you were talking about going to the North Dakota oil fields—ready to do eighty hours? Well, maybe you can house-sit her place. Is that a possibility?" I asked, trying to assist.

"Will you write a letter of recommendation to her for me?"

"No problem. I have written great ones for people looking for work or who were college-bound."

Andrew Carnegie said that if the masses had more money and time, they would just eat and drink more. That isn't all they do, Mr. Carnegie. Should one blame his mother? Something had never been resolved for Brian. He trashed my room. He trashed his life. He always claimed he could complete the project in half the time allotted. He accused his fellows of boondoggling. His nails were always dirty, black underneath, but he showered every day.

CHAPTER TWENTY-NINE
The Sun Will Come Up Again Tomorrow

I, Clancy, the landlord in question, not only lost July rent, but paid $60 to advertise again. COIT, Inc., which advertised with me in my newspaper days, did a beautiful job cleaning the carpet on the stairs, the landings, and the room. Brian would fill his cup with coffee and creamer to the brim, microwave it, and spill it all the way upstairs to his room. Same with soup, etcetera. COIT charged me an additional $68 to deodorize, which didn't stick. Fortunately, the new renter is a smoker—outside, though—so he can't smell it.

I washed the windows, drapes, shower curtain, quilts, bed skirts, the knit sheets Brian left, and my pillows. I threw away his pillows. But there was still a lingering odor. Fortunately, the open window served to camouflage it. The upholstered brown chair with white piping that he sat in all the time must also eventually be subjected to COIT's expertise. He did do a good job of cleaning the bathtub with shower like he said he would. That's as far as he got. I scrubbed again the toilet and sink and treated the drains with Drano.

I took $650 out of savings to amply cover it. At Cleary's Bar and Grill, where I meet friends on some Thursdays, I met Harry's half brother, Charlie, thirty-eight and recently moved here from Maui with his four-year-old son. He had lots of work there by word of mouth until the bottom fell out of the economy in 2008. He said, "I'm a painter, employed."

He offered that he did jobs on weekends and gave free estimates. For $400, Charl masked and spray-painted the entire room and replaced five boards on my back deck that Brian had bounced on and broke; Brian had insisted they were just rotten. Brian weighed two hundred forty pounds or more. He'd said he would replace them. Further, on two walls in my bedroom, Charlie put baseboard molding that I had removed to clean behind. He delivered the decking and molding on Saturday so I could stain them. Sunday he arrived about 10:00 a.m. with his equipment, masked, sprayed two coats, finished, cleaned up, and repacked his pickup by 5:00 p.m. The place looked better than when Brian had arrived. But the odor will drift for a while longer. That's kind of sad.

Charlie shortly designed and built a cupboard with 13 shelves for canned goods for my pantry, painted it white, and installed it for only $100. He was amazing at math, and ultimately his organizational skills and work ethic paid off. Before my story ends, he got a job constructing the only streetcars manufactured in America, with a steel firm in Clackamas. This event necessarily keeps me optimistic and hopeful for my fellows, especially those out of so-called "felony flats." Historians of the area officially designate the flats to be farther west and south, but some longtime inhabitants claim the name for our area, as if we have earned a special destiny.

We're in flux. The immigrants who are optimistic and thankful to be here, away from war and extreme and destructive exclusions, are now graced with an abundance of clean water (or any water), plumbing, vittles, *and* education and jobs. They give my area dignity and unheralded beauty. They tend to keep me on my best outgoing behavior, to set an example. I feel obligated to somehow let them know how great and warm and welcoming our country actually is. I want success for them like I want it for every living soul.

I forced myself to stay positive when I wrote the letter Brian had requested. His request for it made me very sad for a long time. I gave it to him to carry with him to his mother, unsealed. I tend to trust people, give them the benefit of the doubt, unless they give me reason not to trust. So I learn the hard way. There is a lot to learn yet about human nature. Will Brian be welcomed with open arms? He hasn't called. I seriously suspect that eventually I'll make connection with him in North Dakota. He became, all of a sudden, powerless once unemployed, or had he actually been powerless beforehand?

If I had thought it would do any good, I would have told Brian about my mother, who slipped a disc keeping a drunken patient in bed in 1950.

Eventually her left lower leg shriveled and she had to wear a brace for drop foot, just to get in and out of an elevator. She never missed a day of work. A nurse, she was always on her feet forever. She had one beer on hot days while ironing, rum toddies during the holidays, maybe a Manhattan when out to dinner with my grandpa. She never took a pain-killer stronger than Bayer aspirin. Three kids and twenty-three mostly minority employees were dependent on her. She lived to be eighty-four and died with her boots on, on Fourth of July, appropriate since she was a champion of the Bill of Rights, a rooter for human beings. My mom is the reason I bought my wonderful Fourth of July rose climber.

I would tell Brian to "fight it without the pain-killers; the pain is never going to go away no matter how many so-called mendicants you ingest. Marijuana, like sugar, loses its potency, its effect, so you take more and more of it to get any results—and it buries you." But Brian has been in rehab before. He knows all the arguments. My advice would fall on deaf ears. He would just figure I'm shoving an honored citizen up his rear, someone he's not interested in emulating.

If I asked him, "Why don't you see a doctor?" he would say, "No medical insurance, plus an awful diagnosis would affect me on the job, just getting a job." I can hear him now. He'd suffered three weeks with a toothache before the next-door neighbors referred him to a low-cost dentist who was family.

Has Brian become a mere prototype of persons in physically demanding jobs approaching middle age? Brian was a unique heart that suddenly became just ordinary. But if he'd been my son, I would have never given up on him. My mother, widowed in 1945, told us three kids, "You can always come home to me."

I was just another landlord in his life, and logic must prevail, as my son would have said. I must be detached. I had to let him go. My mother is my ideal for what an American ought to be. But I'm a realist, not an idealist. I voted yes for the latest measure on the ballot to legalize marijuana. Ever since I was a child, I was impressed with hemp rope, hemp items. I once ate a brownie mixed with marijuana weed. They were extra chewy, absolutely delicious. It was at a job in 1990 offered by a Palestinian woman who incessantly complained about the Israelis. I didn't have the heart to turn her down and was happy I didn't.

My new renter is a Vietnam veteran, sixty-five years old, diabetic, and just out of rehab. He drives a noisy seventeen-year-old Ford F150 truck with camper, is a finish carpenter, and runs his high-definition television loudly and around the clock. The evidence points to a hard-of-hearing condition, but he claims that's not the case. He insists on adding cable features with Comcast, up to the 700 level now. The bill is up to $109 per month. I had to fight with him to have him pay $85 over rent for the service. In addition, he wants Netflix. "Share, of course," he consistently proposes. For an entire year, he was totally dry and ate three meals per day. A recent hernia operation has "forced" him to imbibe in lots of tequila (in half-gallons he keeps in the freezer) and gallons of margarita mix, which he sometimes adds sugar to. He says he's just on a "downer," that "it's all Agent Orange's fault." Sometimes he pays me $2 for a roll of toilet paper.

Here we go again.

I'm forced to ask the question, "Does 'familiarity breed contempt' or more so, fortuitously provide the basis for the continuation of self preservation?"

Maybe I should do research on how pain (real or conjured) is the greatest motivator for decision making in current American society.

www.ingramcontent.com/pod-product-compliance
Lightning Source LLC
Chambersburg PA
CBHW070914290526
45795CB00001B/319